PRISON BEFORE TRIAL

A study of remand decisions
in magistrates' courts

A. KEITH BOTTOMLEY

Lecturer in Social Administration
University of Hull

OCCASIONAL PAPERS ON SOCIAL ADMINISTRATION NO. 39

*Editorial Committee under the
Chairmanship of Professor R. M. Titmuss*

*Published by G. Bell & Sons,
York House, Portugal Street, Lodon, W.C.2*

First published 1970

ISBN 0 7135 1816 2

MADE AND PRINTED IN ENGLAND BY
WILLMER BROTHERS LIMITED
BIRKENHEAD

FOREWORD

This series of *Occasional Papers* was started in 1960 to supply the need for a medium of publication for studies in the field of social policy and administration which fell between the two extremes of the short article and the full-length book. It was thought that such a series would not only meet a need among research workers and writers concerned with contemporary social issues, but would also strengthen the links between students of the subject and administrators, social workers, committee members and others with responsibilities and interest in the social services.

Contributions to the series should be submitted to the Editorial Committee. A list of earlier papers in this series which are still in print is to be found on the back of this volume.

Richard M. Titmuss

Remand

62
58
60

60 – II

CONTENTS

ACKNOWLEDGEMENTS

The empirical research, which is described in this report, was carried out during 1964–67, while I was a research student at the Institute of Criminology, Cambridge, and formed the basis of a Ph.D. dissertation, submitted to the University of Cambridge in 1969, under the title 'Custodial Remands: a Study of Policy and Practice in Magistrates' Courts'.

It was made possible by the generous cooperation of the Chief Constables of the selected Police Districts, who readily allowed me access to the files I wished to examine, and by the help of the C.I.D. officers and clerical staff, who were more directly involved in the task of tracing the necessary files for me. I must also thank the Clerks to the Justices of the magistrates' courts where observation took place, who were most helpful and friendly to me during my work in their courts, as were members of the local Probation Departments, with whom I had close contact, both in and out of court.

Throughout the research work, I was constantly helped and encouraged by many colleagues at the Institute of Criminology, and also by fellow students at Corpus Christi College, Cambridge. In particular, I owe a great deal to my supervisor, Mr. F. H. McClintock, for the initial encouragement to embark on the research and for his constant help and interest throughout its subsequent stages.

INTRODUCTION

Each year since the middle of the 1960s, in England and Wales, more than 35,000 persons have been remanded in custody before trial. In 1968, which was the first complete year since the passing of the Criminal Justice Act, 1967, with its new restrictions on the refusal of bail, a record total of over 40,000 persons were remanded in custody; more than half of these persons did not subsequently return to prison after conviction, including 2,000 who were found not guilty. The majority of these remand prisoners had been remanded in custody by magistrates' courts in the course of summary proceedings, with only a quarter of them having been committed for trial at a higher court.

Bare statistics like these raise several important questions. How long does a person usually remain in custody before his case is finally heard? How do magistrates decide whether or not a particular defendant should be granted bail? What is the effect upon the prison system of this large category of remand prisoners, and to what extent are they treated differently from convicted prisoners? The first report of the Home Office Research Unit (1960)[1] provided valuable information about the time spent awaiting trial, but there is little systematic information about the decisions made by magistrates, or about the prison experience of persons remanded in custody.

At first sight, it seemed possible that a single research project might combine investigations into these two main areas, but further reflection and the results of a pilot study (Bottomley, 1969, Appendix II), led to the conclusion that no really significant contribution could be made without concentrating upon either one or other of these issues; consequently, the research to be described in the following chapters was directed towards investigating the nature and extent of the decisions of magistrates to remand persons in custody before trial.

1. For References see pp. 115-117.

At the time this research was being planned, a renewed interest in the subject had been created, among English lawyers and criminologists, by research in the United States and Canada (see below, Chapter 3), which indicated that the experience of these countries was perhaps even worse than our own, in terms of the numbers detained before trial and the unsatisfactory operation of their systems for granting bail. It was the development of such interest that contributed directly to the provisions of the Criminal Justice Act, 1967, intended to restrict the circumstances in which magistrates could refuse to grant bail to a defendant.

In this context it was very easy, and all too common, for people in England to ignore many crucial differences in the system of justice as it operated on the other side of the Atlantic, and to assume unquestioningly that the findings of American research would apply equally to the English situation, particularly when these findings appeared to support their own views about the defects of the English system. The views of these critics were many and various: some asserted that the refusal of bail to a defendant before trial was an infringement of the liberty of the individual, and completely alien to the traditional 'presumption of innocence' in the English legal system (e.g. Mostyn, 1964); others protested at the injustice of such large numbers of persons being held in custody before trial, who were subsequently either acquitted or given a non-custodial sentence. Little serious thought was given, for instance, to the relationship between the 'presumption of innocence' and police powers of arrest (Thomas, 1966), or to consideration of the extent to which factors relevant to the sentencing decision were *necessarily* equally relevant to the decision to remand a person in custody.

Other critics have pointed to evidence that a defendant remanded in custody is more likely to plead guilty at his trial; that, if he contests the case, he is more likely to be convicted; and that, on conviction, he is more likely to be sentenced to imprisonment, than is a defendant who has been released on bail. Finally, there were those critics who were concerned not so much with the legal rights of the accused, or the judicial effects of remands in custody, but rather with the personal hardship endured by unconvicted remand prisoners, many of whom were still inadequately segregated in local prisons; and even for those in newer remand centres there were still great inconveniences for consulting with legal advisers, being visited by family and friends, and the risk of losing their jobs.

The practical conclusion of most of these arguments was that many more persons should be granted bail before trial; thus, subsequent debate was mainly centred on the question of *how* more persons could safely be released on bail, rather than on *whether* such release was desirable, and the provisions of the Criminal Justice Act, 1967, were an attempt at devising new regulations for this purpose.

The present research project was planned several years before the Criminal Justice Act, at a time when it was hoped that its findings might be of direct use for future legislation. To some extent, this immediate practical purpose was overtaken by events, although it will be seen that some of the conclusions of the research have been, at least partially, incorporated into the new regulations concerning bail. Nevertheless, there are still many unanswered questions and the system leaves much room for further improvements. The findings described in this report are intended to provide at least partial answers to some of these questions and to suggest possible ways in which remand decisions can be further improved. The social and criminal backgrounds of a sample of persons remanded in custody will be compared with the backgrounds of those released on bail; the processes by which a selected group of magistrates' courts arrived at their remand decisions will be examined; and a critical look taken at comparative research in the United States and Canada, to see what validity it may have for this country. It is only by collecting more information of this kind, and by following up the results of magistrates' decisions, that it will eventually be possible to know whether or not too many persons, or the wrong persons, are being remanded in custody, and to know how to improve the quality of decision-making in magistrates' courts.

1. DETENTION BEFORE TRIAL IN ENGLAND: THE BACKGROUND

Segregation and Privileges of Untried Prisoners

The prisons of England and Wales have always contained a large number of unconvicted persons awaiting trial. In fact, before the middle of the nineteenth century, when transportation came to an end and the number of capital offences was drastically reduced, the detention of untried prisoners was perhaps the commonest single function of the gaols throughout the country (Pugh, 1968; Webbs, 1922). It is therefore not altogether surprising that the feature of contemporary prisons, in 1773, which first stimulated John Howard to begin his famous investigation into prison conditions at home and abroad was the plight of the untried prisoners, and he soon brought sharply to public notice evidence of the lack of any kind of segregation in most gaols, whether by sex, age, criminal sophistication or the fact of being untried.

Howard's report, *The State of the Prisons* (1777), influenced legislation during the last quarter of the eighteenth century, which attempted to ensure that all prisoners should be kept in separate cells, to eliminate the evils inherent in the existing lack of segregation. Unfortunately this attempt to ease conditions for untried prisoners did not prove to be practicable or popular, and was later superceded by the provisions of Peel's 1823 Prisons Act, which introduced the new principle of the classification of prisoners, involving separate classes for unconvicted 'felons and misdemeanants'.

Once again it proved impossible to enforce this legislation, and the movement of official opinion in the 1830s, influenced by developments in America, was towards favouring the idea of separate confinement of prisoners. The Prisons Act of 1839 repealed the previous legislation advocating classification, and in its place gave approval to the principle of separate confinement. This principle shaped the physical structure of the 'model prison' built at Pentonville in 1842 and of the massive prison building programme of the next two decades. Consequently, the wholesale acceptance of the principle of separate confinement of prisoners at this time not only closed the door for a long time on further public debate about the special needs of various classes of prisoner but left future generations with a legacy of prison buildings which could not be easily adapted to any new ideas, which might eventually be considered more appropriate for unconvicted prisoners.

Gradually, in the course of the nineteenth century, a number of special privileges were accorded to untried prisoners, so that by 1877 the basis had been firmly laid for most of the privileges which (at least theoretically) can be exercised by them today. In 1865 the administration and discipline of prisons had been tightened, and the Prisons Act of that year specified that untried prisoners were to be separated from the convicted, that they were to be allowed to obtain their own food, clothing and bedding, at their own expense, and that they may be allowed to work (DuCane, 1885). These provisions were consolidated by the Prisons Act, 1877, which required the Secretary of State to make special rules 'in such manner as to make it as little as possible oppressive, due regard only being had to their safe custody, to the necessity of preserving order and good government in the place in which they are confined, and to the physical and moral well-being of the prisoners themselves'; these rules were to allow (1) retaining possession of books and papers, which were not required for evidence, (2) private communication with friends and legal advisers, (3) the provision of their own food, and (4) no compulsion to work against their own will. This legislation provided the basis at the end of the nineteenth century, and, with some slight additions, up to the present time.

The official handbook, *Prisons and Borstals,* discusses the category of untried prisoners in very similar terms to the 1877 Act:

> The conditions of their confinement therefore must secure safe-custody and supervision in no less a degree than for convicted prisoners... Subject to these conditions, the treatment of this class should be as little as possible oppressive or restrictive. (Home Office, 1960, p.38)

It proceeds to describe their present position 'so far as possible separated from all other classes of prisoner', and emphasises the privileges of being allowed to wear their own clothes, of not being compelled to work, buying their own food, and paying for special rooms and facilities. They are allowed more frequent letters and visits than convicted prisoners, and are given proper facilities for private meetings with legal advisers.

The culmination of the trends towards increased segregation and privileges for untried prisoners, which have been briefly outlined in this introductory section, was the introduction of remand centres in the early 1960s. The first official reference to the intention of providing special remand centres was in the Criminal Justice Act,

1948, but the first centre did not materialize until 1961, when Ashford Remand Centre, Middlesex, was opened, for young men under the age of 21 years, awaiting trial or sentence.

Following this first experiment, the Prison Department went ahead with a considerable building programme for more remand centres, and acheived their aim of having a total of nine new or newly converted centres in operation by the end of 1965. Three were opened in 1964, at Winchester, Cardiff and Exeter, for young men under the age of twenty-one, and five more followed in 1965, at Thorp Arch, Risley, Brockhill, Low Newton and Pucklechurch. The last four included provision for girls under the age of twenty-one, and Risley had comprehensive provision for adults and young persons of both sexes.

Thus, by the end of 1965, the Prison Department was able to announce that 17 per cent of all adult prisoners on remand, and 80 per cent of persons under the age of twenty-one were held in remand centres; this still meant that 60 per cent of all remand prisoners were in local prisons, mainly in the areas not covered by remand centres, which included East Anglia, the east and south-east Midlands, Kent and Sussex. Finally, in 1967, a part of Holloway prison was converted for use as a remand centre for girls, and plans were in the design stage for extensions or new centres to provide accommodation for another 332 remand prisoners.

Very little is known about the actual experience of untried prisoners in custody, as to whether or to what extent they take advantage of the privileges available to them, about the realities of segregation in local prisons, or how they react to their time in custody before trial. When the research was being planned, the feasibility of trying to answer some of these questions was considered, and a small pilot survey of a group of borstal inmates was carried out. Although it was subsequently decided that it was not possible to pursue this particular approach, some interesting points emerged which indicated that future research in this area might reveal unexpected findings.[1]

The survey was conducted in the early months of 1965, when 60 per cent of the sample had been awaiting trial in remand centres and 40 per cent in local prisons, enabling comparisons to be made of their respective experiences. By definition, remand centres kept the boys segregated from sentenced prisoners, but, even in the local prisons with their problems of Victorian architecture and chronic overcrowding, when they were unconvicted half the boys were in landings only housing other untried prisoners, and less than a fifth were on the same landing as any category of sentenced prisoner.

1. For a full report of this survey, see A. K. Bottomley, *Custodial Remands: a Study of Policy and Practice in Magistrates' Courts*, (Unpublished Ph.D. thesis, Cambridge University, 1969) Appendix II. For the experiences of over 400 prisoners in Risley Remand Centre, see C. Davies, *Imprisonment before Sentence*, (Unpublished M. A. thesis, University of Liverpool, 1968).

Most of these boys wanted to work on remand, as their main single complaint about the experience was boredom, but 36 per cent in local prisons were not provided with work, compared to less than 5 per cent in remand centres.

Despite the fact that Prison Rules allow untried prisoners to have daily visits, yet 60 per cent of the boys in remand centres had no visits at all, compared to 27 per cent in local prisons, and over half in prisons were visited at least once a week, compared to a third of the boys in remand centres. It is difficult to explain these differences, particularly as the remand centres were no further from the boys' homes than were the prisons, but there are, of course, many other reasons why untried prisoners who are later sentenced to borstal training may not have had many visits. All interviews with their legal advisers, police and probation officers, were conducted in private rooms 'in the sight, but not in the hearing' of a prison officer.

Finally, when questioned about their general reaction to the remand experience (being in a position to compare it retrospectively with their periods at allocation centre and borstal), over half of those in remand centres showed a favourable reaction, compared to only a quarter in prisons. Inasmuch as four out of every five boys detained in remand centres were content with, or at least indifferent to, their conditions and surroundings, it would seem to vindicate the Prison Department's recent policy whereby 80 per cent of this age group are now in remand centres.

Prison Statistics

In 1877 the central government took control of all prisons in England and Wales, and it marks a convenient date from which to examine available information about the number of untried prisoners held in custody, as this centralization meant that national statistics began to be published in the annual *Reports of the Commissioners of Prisons.*

Throughout the last quarter of the nineteenth century and the beginning of the twentieth, up to the 1914–18 war, the total number of persons received into prisons each year averaged between 175,000 –215,000, and, of this annual total, between 20,000—25,000 were unconvicted prisoners awaiting trial. Table 1 shows the figures for this period, which confirm that more than one in ten of the prisoners received each year were untried. Approximately half these prisoners had been committed for trial to Assizes or Quarter Sessions, and about a sixth of this group were subsequently acquitted.

For the first five years after the post-war return of a more normal publication of prison statistics, in 1921, the only information about untried prisoners that was published was the number who were not later received into prison on sentence (i.e. they were either acquitted or given a sentence other than one of imprisonment). This number was as high as 10,300 in 1921, dropping to 7,000 by 1925.

Annual figures of prison receptions were published again from 1926: the total number was down to 60,000—less than a third of the figures for the pre-war period. During the next twenty years, prison receptions dropped to below 50,000 each year, but the proportion of the total who were untried prisoners not later sentenced to imprisonment increased to over one fifth, including a significant number who were found not guilty.

Table 1

Annual Prison Receptions of Untried Prisoners, 1879–1911

	Annual Averages		
	1879–1889	*1890–1899*	*1900–1911*
Total prison receptions	182,743	175,859	209,477
Untried prisoners			
(i) remanded and tried summarily	10,721	10,951	12,557
(ii) committed for trial to higher courts	12,597	10,046	10,561
Total untried	23,318	20,997	23,557
(% of all receptions)	(12.8)	(11.9)	(11.0)

Source: *Reports of the Commissioners of Prisons, 1879–1911,* Appendix I.

After the Second World War there was no immediate increase in the number of prison receptions, which remained at around 50,000, until 1952, when there was a sudden increase to over 75,000 and for the first time for more than forty years the *total* number of prisoners awaiting trial was published. In 1952, a third of all prison receptions were unconvicted and awaiting trial, and by the end of the 1950s, when the annual receptions had risen to nearly 90,000 almost 30,000 were unconvicted, of whom 40 per cent did not subsequently return to prison after conviction.

In 1960 there was a reorganization of prison statistics, which resulted in better information about untried prisoners. Between 1960–67, the total number of persons received into prison each year gradually increased, until it reached almost 124,000 in 1966 and 1967. In 1968, when most of the provisions of the Criminal Justice Act, 1967, expected to reduce the prison population, came into full effect, the number of receptions went down to 116,000. Table 2 shows the main statistical details for this recent period.

The total of untried prisoners (not including s.26 remands[1]) remained fairly constantly around 30,000 until after 1965, so that this group formed only 25 per cent of all receptions in 1965, compared

1. Since 1961, persons remanded for medical reports (by s.26 of the Magistrates' Courts Act, 1952) have been included in the class of 'untried prisoners' in Table C.1 of the *Statistical Tables*, and therefore included in the statistics of untried prisoners 'who did not subsequently return to prison on conviction'. Exact comparisons with earlier years are therefore not possible.

to over 30 per cent in 1961. However, in 1966 the number of untried prisoners suddenly increased to over 35,000, and this increase continued into 1968, despite the new provisions (Criminal Justice Act, 1967) restricting the refusal of bail, when the total of 37,000 untried prisoners constituted 32 per cent of all prison receptions. Not only was this proportion higher than in any year since 1959, but in 1968 more than half these prisoners were not returned to prison after conviction (including 5 per cent who were acquitted), which is the largest proportion recorded this century.

TABLE 2

Annual Prison Receptions of Untried Prisoners, 1961-68.

	1961	*1963*	*1965*	*1967*	*1968*
Total prison receptions	98,266	116,082	114,488	123,834	116,036
Untried prisoners					
(a) Under age of 21	8,424	8,481	8,189	11,888	11,939
(b) 21 years and over	22,023	23,676	20,432	24,752	25,238
Total	30,447	32,157	28,621	36,640	37,177
(% of all receptions)	(31·0)	(27·7)	(25·5)	(29·6)	(31·9)
TOTAL (inc. s.26 remands)	33,545	35,506	33,999	40,262	40,503
(i) acquitted	1,390	1,449	2,075	2,590	1,997
(%)	(4·1)	(4·1)	(6·1)	(6·9)	(4·9)
(ii) non-custodial sentence	12,823	14,698	13,883	15,541	19,158
(%)	(38·3)	(41·4)	(40·8)	(38·6)	(47·3)

Source: *Report of the Commissioners of Prisons, 1961; Reports on the Work of the Prison Department, 1963–68, Statistical Tables.*

A final point to be noted is that the problems posed for the administration and organization of prisons by untried prisoners result as much from the very rapid transfer and movements of this group as from the actual amount of prison accommodation which they occupy at any one time. If the daily average prison *population* is considered, it is found that, since the Second World War, untried prisoners have usually constituted only 5 per cent of the prison population; even in 1968, untried prisoners only constituted 5.4 per cent of the daily average prison population.

The granting of bail

In the final section of this chapter, the focus of attention will be turned from statistics of persons remanded in custody before trial, to a consideration of what information is available about the number released on bail. The only regularly published statistics are contained in the annual volume of *Criminal Statistics, England and Wales*, but they do not provide anything like a complete picture, as they only refer to persons who are committed for trial to Assizes and Quarter Sessions, and give no information about the larger number of persons who are remanded in the course of summary trial in magistrates' courts.

The annual volume of *Criminal Statistics* first appeared in a form similar to that of the present day following the major reorganization in 1893 of what were then called the *Judicial Statistics.* The revised *Criminal Statistics* gave information, derived from police returns of indictable offences, of all persons committed for trial in each of six main offence classes, showing the numbers of those committed in custody and those released on bail. In 1893, for example, the 10,000 persons remanded in custody after committal for trial represented 80 per cent of all persons committed for trial, as only 20 per cent were granted bail.

In the course of the next twenty years, it has already been noted that the number committed for trial in custody remained at around 10,000 each year; the *Criminal Statistics* show that the proportion released on bail remained fairly constant, so that although there was a slight increase towards the end of the period, yet over three-quarters were still remanded in custody in 1913. The proportions released on bail in each of the main offence groups remained surprisingly consistent: in Class 1 (Offences against the person) approximately one-third were always released on bail, whereas in Class 2 (Offences against property with violence) never more than one in ten were granted bail.

In the inter-war years the proportion of persons who were committed for trial on bail slowly increased, until by 1938 nearly six out of ten persons were granted bail. Since 1945, the proportion of persons committed for trial who have been released on bail remained fairly constantly around 60 per cent, althought the most recent figures for 1968 show that nearly 70 per cent were released on bail in that year (Table 3).

TABLE 3

Percentage of persons in each offence class committed for trial on bail, 1946–1968.

	1946	*1955*	*1965*	*1968*
Class I (Offences against the person) (no.)	73·0 (2,246)	72·1 (3,106)	72·2 (3,946)	73·0 (4,671)
Class II (Offences against property, with violence)	54·2 (5,853)	44·7 (4,132)	48·6 (5,955)	58·6 (8,651)
Class III (Offences against property without violence)	67·7 (2,428)	76·4 (2,253)	79·7 (4,514)	84·4 (6,350)
Class IV (Malicious damage to property)	55·6 (49)	45·0 (72)	50·1 (166)	61·4 (296)
Class V (Forgery and currency offences)	58·7 (174)	85·3 (246)	74·5 (224)	79·0 (412)
Class VI (Other indictable offences)	93·6 (203)	86·9 (172)	85·3 (498)	89·1 (417)
TOTAL (no.)	60·9 (11,222)	57·7 (9,981)	62·2 (15,303)	69·0 (20,797)

Source: *Criminal Statistics, England and Wales, 1946–1968.*

This is not the place for a detailed examination of the differences in the proportions granted bail in various offence groups (see below, pp 75ff.), but it is perhaps appropriate at this point to indicate that the overall totals of the six main classes often conceal a considerable range of variations within each class. This variation is particularly evident in 'Offences against the person' (Class I) and in 'Offences against property without violence' (Class III). For example, in cases of 'murder of persons over the age of one year' usually only one per cent of persons are granted bail, compared to 98 or 99 per cent in 'causing death by dangerous driving'; similarly, in offences of 'larceny in a dwelling-house' usually only about half the persons are granted bail, whereas in 'embezzlement' more than nine out of ten are granted bail on committal for trial.

The fact that the *Criminal Statistics* do not provide any information about the extent to which magistrates' courts release on bail or remand in custody persons who are tried summarily is an obvious and serious limitation, which prevents administrators and research workers from having any regular information about court remand practice. Even the information which *is* provided is very 'static', in that there is no attempt to relate it to the eventual outcome of the trial. This is a particularly important gap in our knowledge, in view of the concern expressed recently, especially in the United States, about the possible effect that being remanded in custody might have upon the outcome of the trial (see below, Chapter 3)

In default of adequate information from the annually published official statistics, the most useful data comes from the research carried out by the Home Office Research Unit, which published the findings in its report, *Time Spent Awaiting Trial* (1960). This report provided an instructive framework for the present research, and will be frequently referred to in later chapters.

The main purpose of the Home Office research was to discover the time spent awaiting trial by defendants, but in the course of this investigation valuable information was provided about the use of remands by magistrates' courts, and about differences between those released on bail and those detained in custody. One part of the survey covered a representative sample of one hundred magistrates' courts, which dealt with over a third of all persons appearing at magistrates' courts in England and Wales. During April, 1958, 935 persons were remanded before conviction by the courts in the sample, tried summarily and sentenced by the magistrates: 64 per cent were released on bail for all the time before trial, and 30 per cent were remanded in custody all the time. Slightly over half of the persons (54 per cent) who were convicted after being remanded in custody were not given a custodial sentence by the magistrates.

The next chapter will describe the special practices of selected magistrates' courts in England, during 1963–66, in an attempt to provide some more recent information about court practices, and to provide a framework for the observation of the decision-making process, which formed a central part of the empirical work.

2. A SURVEY OF VARIATIONS IN URBAN AND RURAL COURT PRACTICE.

Selection of Courts and Sample

It has been seen, in the previous chapter, that there is no regularly published information, in the *Criminal Statistics* or elsewhere, which enables comparisons to be made between the remand practices of different courts or between courts in different types of area. There are not even any regular statistics kept at the local level (by the courts or the police) of the frequency of remands at magistrates' courts, which might provide a sampling frame, from which a properly representative sample of courts could be drawn. Indeed, the only way to discover this information is to consult the daily register compiled by the Clerk to the Court.

Previous research into the sentencing policy of magistrates courts has shown that certain differences are associated with the socio-economic characteristics of the community served by the particular court, including such factors as population density, crime rate and social class distribution.[1] It therefore seemed a likely hypothesis, for the present research, that if the courts to be studied were selected from such different types of area then any differences that might exist in the practice of remanding persons in custody before trial would be brought to light. An associated factor, which also seemed likely to affect a court's remand practice was the frequency of its regular court sittings.

Various practical considerations limited the number of courts which could be studied, so that the final selection of courts was (a) an urban court in the North of England, serving a city with a population of approximately 300,000 and dealing with an annual average of 1,800 indictable offenders (over the age of 17); and (b) three rural courts in East Anglia, serving a total population of approximately 40,000 (within the same Police District), and dealing with an annual average of 200 indictable offenders. The urban court sat

1. See especially R. G. Hood, *Sentencing in Magistrates' Courts*, (London, 1962) Chapter 5; also M. Grünhut, *Juvenile Offenders Before the Courts*, (Oxford, 1956), and K. W. Patchett and J. D. McClean 'Decision-making in Juvenile Cases', [1965] *Crim. L.R.* 699.

on six days each week, but the rural courts each sat on only one day of the week[1].

The remand practice of these courts was studied in two complementary ways. Observation of actual decision-making by the magistrates was undertaken for consecutive periods during 1965 and 1966[2]; this forms the basis of the findings to be described in Chapters 4 and 5. Secondly, the frequency of remands at these courts was studied from the court registers, and samples of remanded persons were selected for special study[2]; the main findings of this part of the investigation will be described in the present chapter and Chapter 6.

Before describing the selection of the sample of remanded persons, it may be helpful at this stage to clarify the various types of remand which are possible in magistrates' courts. In cases of indictable offences (or offences triable either on indictment or summarily, where the court has begun to hear the case as an indictable offence), when the proceedings before the magistrates' courts have to be adjourned the accused must be remanded. In all other offences the power of magistrates to remand the accused is discretionary, and it is usual for him to be informed of the new date for the adjourned hearing. When an accused is remanded, he must either be detained in custody or released on bail (with or without sureties) for his appearance at the adjourned hearing.

A remand can be either before or after conviction. If it is before conviction it is either:

(a) when the case is adjourned to be heard before the magistrates at a later date (when in custody, such a remand cannot exceed eight days at a time); or

(b) when the accused is committed for trial to a higher court.

If a remand is *after* conviction, it is either:

(c) so that the magistrates can obtain probation, medical or other reports to assist them in sentencing (by s.14.3 or s.26 of the Magistrates' Courts Act, 1952); or

(d) when the accused is committed for sentence to Quarter Sessions, after being convicted by the magistrates (by s.28 or s.29 of the Magistrates' Courts Act, 1952).

At the time of the research, only remands in the last category (d) had to be in custody; in all other categories the magistrates exercised complete discretion to remand either in custody or on bail. The Criminal Justice Act, 1967, s.20 made it also discretionary

1. Throughout the rest of the report these courts will usually simply be referred to as (a) the urban court, and (b) the rural courts; this shorthand form of reference is not meant to imply that they are necessarily 'typical' or representative of urban and rural courts, because, as we have seen, there is no way of knowing their representativeness.
2. Further methodological details will be found in the Appendix.

whether a remand by s.28 or s.29 of the Magistrates' Courts Act, 1952, was on bail or in custody.

The first step in the sampling procedure was that the persons appearing at the urban and rural courts, charged with indictable offences, were divided into three groups as follows:[1]

Group A—Violence against the person;
Group B—Larceny and False Pretences;
Group C—Breaking and Entering Offences.

The number of persons remanded in each group during 1964 was recorded, but in order to obtain enough cases from the rural courts, the survey in these courts had to be extended to the three-year period, 1963–65. The figures of persons remanded are shown in Table 4. In both the urban and the rural courts, just over one-third of all persons were remanded at their first court appearance, but the proportions varied according to the offence group, with most remanded in Group C (Breaking and Entering) and the least in group B (Larceny and False Pretences).

TABLE 4

Proportions of persons, in each offence group, remanded at the urban and rural courts

	Urban Court (1964)			*Rural Courts (1963–65)*		
	Total	Remanded		*Total*	Remanded	
		no.	%		no.	%
Group A (Violence against the person)	135	57	42·2	39	18	46·2
Group B (Larceny and False Pretences)	1,026	278	27·0	448	116	25·8
Group C (Breaking and Entering)	606	303	50·0	112	79	70·5
TOTAL	1,767	638	36·1	599	213	35·5

It was estimated that the size of the sample of remanded persons which could be adequately investigated was approximately 400 persons, divided equally between the urban and the rural courts. In the light of the number of persons remanded at the selected courts (Table 4), it was decided that the sample should include:

(a) all the 213 persons remanded at the rural courts, 1963–65;
(b) all the persons in Group A, remanded at the urban court, 1964;
(c) a 25 per cent random sample of persons in Groups B and C, remanded at the urban court, 1964.

This gave a total of 203 persons from the urban court, and a final basic sample of 416 persons.

1. See the Appendix for details of the offences included in each of these three groups.

Because of the different sampling proportions in Groups B and C, at the urban and rural courts, in those parts of the subsequent analysis which involve comparisons between the urban and rural samples the urban statistics have been 'reweighted', so that each offence group constitutes its proper proportion of the total. Table 5 shows how the final sample was made up.

TABLE 5

Distribution of selected sample of offenders, remanded at the urban and rural courts

	Total Sample		*Urban Court (1964)*		*Rural Courts (1963–65)*
Group A (Violence against the person)	75		57		18
Group B (Larceny and False Pretences)	186	(396)*	70	(280)*	116
Group C (Breaking and Entering)	155	(383)	76	(304)	79
TOTAL	416	(854)	203	(641)	213

* The figures in brackets are reweighted, to take account of the different sampling proportions.

Before the main analysis of the frequency and length of the remands in the sample is described, brief consideration will be given to the preliminary procedures of summons and arrest, whereby the persons first appeared in court before being remanded by the magistrates.

Summons and Arrest

If all persons were summonsed to appear before the magistrates, instead of being arrested, a large majority of remands before conviction would be unnecessary. Very little information is available about the use of the summons in England and Wales, but a few interesting facts have emerged from this present research, which emphasize the relationship between the use of summons by the police and remand decisions by the magistrates.

In his survey of 6,000 offences, heard in the Toronto Magistrates' Courts, 1961–2, Martin L. Friedland (1965) found that in slightly over 92 per cent of the cases the accused was arrested, and 'there was an insignificant variation between the use of the summons for indictable and non-indictable offences; in both, arrests were made in approximately 92 per cent of the cases'. Friedland compared this situation with that which existed in England, basing his comparison on the figures available in the *Criminal Statistics, England and Wales*. He found that the proportion of arrests was consistently very much higher in Toronto than it was in England, and rejected the theory that a possible explanation for this would be that he was comparing a large urban area with statistics for a whole country:

> Any comparison between national figures and those for a large metropolitan area, such as Toronto, must take into account possible differences between urban and rural practices. The figures (of persons summonsed) for the large urban centres in England may be somewhat lower than the national figures, but there is no reason to believe they are significantly different. There is no suggestion in the literature that the general procedures for compelling the accused's appearance in court differ in various parts of the country, nor is there any indication that the summons is infrequently used in the larger cities.
>
> (Friedland, 1965, p.12)

However, the small amount of relevant data from the urban and rural courts in this survey suggest that there is, in fact, considerable difference in the police procedures for ensuring the accused's appearance in courts, between the urban and rural areas, and that this difference is subsequently reflected in the decision of the court when remanding the accused, on bail or in custody.

Friedland's statistics for English practice were derived from *Criminal Statistics, England and Wales,* 1961, Table 1. Since the introduction of computer processing by the Home Office, in 1964, the annual *Criminal Statistics* have provided more information than before, especially with regard to the classification by age of persons proceeded against. In 1968, 73 per cent of all persons proceeded against for indictable offences, in England and Wales, were arrested, and 27 per cent were summonsed to appear before the magistrates. If persons under the age of 17 are excluded from the calculation, it is found that four-fifths of indictable offenders (aged seventeen or over) were arrested, and only one-fifth summonsed.

In the preliminary stages of sampling the remand cases from the urban and rural courts, a record was made of all the indictable offenders (aged seventeen and over) proceeded against in the three offence groups, during the years which were being studied. In the urban court register an entry was always made as to whether the offender was proceeded against by arrest or summons, and thus it was possible to examine the use of the summons in this court during 1964. Unfortunately, only one of the three rural courts recorded such information in its register and so it was not possible to obtain a complete picture of practice throughout the rural courts.

The total number of persons in the three offence groups appearing at the urban court in 1964 was 1,767: the proportion proceeded against by summons was 21 per cent, almost identical to the national average. The total number of persons appearing at the one rural court, 1963–65, was 163, of whom a much greater proportion of 36 per cent were summonsed. In the urban court, the summons was virtually non-existent for 'breaking and entering' offences, as only 2 out of the 606 persons in this group were summonsed, compared to three out of the forty-two in the rural court. In both courts, most of the indictable offenders who were summonsed were in Group B (Larceny and False Pretences): in the urban court they constituted 88 per cent of the total summonsed, and in the rural court 86 per cent.

A slightly different approach was to analyse the sample of remanded persons according to how they were initially proceeded against by the police. When this was done, it was found that as many as one-fifth of the rural cases were summonsed, whereas in the urban sample less than 2 per cent were proceeded against by summons. Apart from the much greater proportion of the remand cases summonsed to appear at the rural courts, there were other differences in the circumstances under which the accused persons appeared before the magistrates who remanded them. In the urban court, 80 per cent of the sample appeared in police custody, having been arrested the previous day and having spent a night in police cells; only 40 per cent of the rural cases had spent the previous night in police cells. Almost 11 per cent of the urban cases had been arrested and bailed to appear at court by the police, compared to over 18 per cent who had been bailed by the police to appear at the rural courts.

There was a very strong relationship between the initial police action in ensuring the accused's appearance at court, and the outcome of the first court appearance, in terms of whether he was remanded on bail or in custody: of the persons who appeared in direct police custody (i.e. after overnight custody, or arrest the same day), 83 per cent of those in the urban court and 90 per cent of those in the rural courts were remanded in custody; but, of the persons who had been released on bail by the police, 92 per cent were remanded on bail by the magistrates.

One of the differences between the urban and rural courts was that in the urban court more of those who appeared in direct police custody were then remanded on bail than was the case in the rural courts: thus, more than 40 per cent of those remanded on bail by the urban court had been in police custody overnight, compared to less than 10 per cent of those remanded on bail by the rural courts; and, conversely, only 1 per cent of those remanded in custody by the urban court had *not* appeared in police custody, compared to 14 per cent of those remanded in custody by the rural courts.

Finally, more than 90 per cent of the persons summonsed at the urban courts were remanded on bail, compared to 75 per cent of those summonsed at the rural courts.

Many arguments levelled against an excessive use of arrest and police custody, instead of summons and police bail, are the same as those used against unnecessary remands in custody by magistrates, once the accused has appeared in court. Friedland sees the police arrest procedure essentially as one for the convenience of the police in carrying out their investigation:

> The arrest and detention of accused persons makes the work of the police easier in at least two ways: the police have the opportunity of questioning the accused and obtaining a confession, and they know that, whether or not the accused is questioned, he is more likely to plead guilty the next morning if he is kept in custody rather than if he is initially summonsed. Custody in order psychologically to induce guilty pleas is obviously not proper. Detention for questioning is the crux of the problem. . . .
>
> (Friedland, 1965, p.40)

Assuming these findings concerning the greater use of the summons in the rural courts may be valid for the country as a whole, the two most obvious explanations would seem to be that, in the first place, the urgency of the crime problem may be much less serious in the rural areas than in the cities, so that the summons is seen as the appropriate method of police procedure in more cases; and, in the second place, the fact that rural courts only sit on one or two days of the week (or less frequently) means that if the police arrest a suspect and wish to keep him in custody, they must often arrange a special court hearing, which causes considerable inconvenience to all the personnel involved, and is avoided if the police believe that an alternative procedure will suffice, in the best interests of justice.

Remands before conviction or committal for trial

More than 95 per cent of the urban cases and 80 per cent of the rural were remanded at least once before being convicted by the magistrates or committed for trial to a higher court. The rural courts committed for trial rather more of their cases than the urban court (36 per cent compared to 29 per cent), with correspondingly fewer tried and sentenced by the magistrates (55 per cent compared to 64 per cent). From the documentation available in the police files of the urban cases, it was possible to examine the main reasons for these initial remands in the urban court.

The majority of remands (56 per cent) were for further police enquiries, especially in 'breaking and entering' offences (Group C) and larcenies (Group B), where the numbers of remands for this reason were 71 per cent and 65 per cent respectively. These police enquiries were usually quite specific, and often resulted in either additional charges and offences 'taken into consideration', or in the subsequent arrest and joint trial of all the offenders suspected of being involved in the offence (see below, pp 80ff.).

In cases of violence (Group A) the accused was not so often remanded for police enquiries (25 per cent), but more often the case had to be adjourned until important witnesses or the complainant himself had recovered from injuries, to enable them to testify (29 per cent).

A significant minority of remands were requested by the defendant (7 per cent), either so that he could obtain legal aid or to enable his solicitor to have more time to prepare the defence. Over 90 per cent of the remands in this group resulted in bail being granted.

A comparison of the total length of time for which persons were remanded before conviction or committal for trial shows a pattern which, in most respects, appears very similar in the urban and rural courts. The average time was 11–12 days: remands entirely in custody averaged 8 days, those entirely on bail 14–16 days.

Comparing the urban and the rural cases, not only was the length of time very similar, but so were the proportions on bail and in custody: 61 per cent of the urban and 56 per cent of the rural were remanded entirely in custody; 30 per cent of the urban and 31 per cent of the rural cases were remanded entirely on bail. The main differences between the urban and the rural cases was that in the former there were more remanded in custody for a very short time: 30 per cent of those remanded in custody before conviction by the urban court were detained for 48 hours or less, compared to 13 per cent by the rural courts.

However, when the same cases were divided into those who were tried summarily and those who were committed for trial, one or two differences between the urban and rural cases did then emerge.

In the cases which were tried summarily, the urban court remanded 60 per cent in custody, compared to 45 per cent at the rural courts; and the rural courts released 44 per cent on bail, compared to only 31 per cent at the urban court.

There were also differences in the length of time spent on remand by persons who were eventually committed for trial: in the urban court the average was twenty-five days, more than twice as long as in the rural courts, where the average was twelve days. This finding, together with the fact that a greater proportion of those committed for trial at the rural courts were committed at their first court appearance than at the urban court (16 per cent compared to less than 5 per cent), suggests that the greater pressure of police and court work in the city meant that committal proceedings took longer to arrange and prepare. Thus, although summary trial was slightly quicker in the urban court (for those who had to be remanded), committal proceedings usually took longer to arrange than in the rural courts. In the next section it will be seen that the time spent awaiting trial *after* committal was also longer for the urban cases than for the rural.

Committals for trial

Sixty per cent of the persons committed for trial by the urban court were committed in custody, and 40 per cent were committed on bail; in the rural courts only 46 per cent were committed in custody and 54 on bail. Not only were more persons committed in custody by the urban court, but on average they had to wait ten days longer than their counterparts at the rural courts (35 days compared to 25 days). Comparing the length of time spent waiting trial by those in custody with that of those on bail shows the usual pattern whereby those on bail waited longer than those in custody.

Just as a strong relationship was found between whether a person appeared in police custody and whether he was subsequently remanded in custody by the magistrates, so there was an equally strong relationship between whether a person was initially remanded in custody and whether he was subsequently committed for trial in custody. In the rural courts, none of those committed for trial in custody had been remanded on bail; and, in the urban court, less than 4 per cent of those committed in custody had been remanded on bail. Conversely, only 14 per cent of those committed on bail at the rural courts had been previously remanded in custody, although as many as 45 per cent of those committed on bail by the urban court had been previously remanded in custody. Expressed in a slightly different way, in the rural courts all those persons committed for trial, who had been remanded on bail for all or part of the time before committal, were also committed for trial on bail; and only 11 per cent of those previously remanded in custody all the time were subsequently committed for trial on bail. Similarly, in the urban court, less than 9 per cent of the persons previously remanded on bail for all or part of the time were committed for trial in custody; and only one-fifth of those who had been remanded in custody all the time were subsequently committed for trial on bail.

Summary

This necessary, if rather statistical, examination of the practice at the urban and rural courts selected for study has revealed certain features which may indicate real differences in the practice of similar courts throughout the country.

The initial decision of the police, whether to proceed against a person suspected of an indictable offence by means of a summons or by arrest, seemed to be influenced by the type of area in which they operated. Process by summons was more common in the rural courts, although it is difficult to know how much this was due to the different crime situation in the rural area or how much to the relative infrequency of court sittings. There were considerable differences in practice even after the police had initially arrested a suspect: in the rural area almost a quarter were then released on police bail until the court hearing, compared to only 11 per cent in the urban area; and, whereas at the urban court, this meant that over 80 per cent of those who had been arrested spent the night before their court appearance in police custody, yet only half those arrested in the rural area spent the night in police custody.

These findings have an added significance because of the apparent association between this initial police action and the subsequent decision by the magistrates to remand in custody or on bail; this association meant that, of persons appearing in court in police custody, 83 per cent of those in the urban court and 90 per cent of those in the rural courts were remanded in custody, whereas over 90 per cent of persons who had been bailed by the police were also granted bail by the magistrates. Obviously, this kind of association may mean nothing more than that the police and the magistrates use similar criteria in reaching their decisions, and not that the earlier police decision has any independent influence upon the court decision, but until more evidence has been collected neither of these interpretations can be definitely confirmed or rejected.

At the first appearance in court, it was found that just over a a third of persons charged with indictable offences in both the urban and the rural courts were not dealt with immediately, but were remanded by the magistrates or committed for trial. The average length of time, in all the courts, for which persons were remanded before conviction or committal for trial was eight days, for those in custody, and fourteen to sixteen days for those on bail; but the urban court more frequently remanded persons for 48 hours or less, than did the rural courts.

Finally, considering the remands before conviction of those persons who were tried summarily, more were remanded in custody at the urban court than at the rural, although the time spent in custody was on average four days less; on the other hand, the persons who were eventually committed for trial by the magistrates at the urban court had to wait twice as long *before* committal, than at the rural courts, and when they were committed for trial more persons were again committed in custody and also had to wait longer for trial than persons committed by the rural courts.

3. THE EFFECTS OF CUSTODIAL REMANDS: COMPARATIVE EVIDENCE

Recent research carried out in the United States of America and Canada has revealed apparent associations between remands in custody and the outcome of the trial; it has been suggested that persons who are remanded in custody before trial are more likely to be found guilty than persons released on bail, and also that they are more likely to be sentenced to a term of imprisonment than persons who are released on bail before trial. This chapter takes a critical look at some of this research material, and in the light of new evidence from the English courts studied suggests modifications to the usual interpretations of the facts.

The likelihood of conviction

The first finding which will be examined is that persons remanded in custody before trial are more likely to be found guilty than are persons released on bail.

The University of Pennsylvania Law School, under the direction of Caleb Foote, studied 946 cases remanded before trial in Philadelphia during October and November, 1953, (Foote, Markle & Woolley, 1954). An initial analysis showed that 48 per cent of persons on bail were not convicted, compared to only 18 per cent of those in custody. When offenders were divided into offence groups, this difference was not so consistently found: in the case of persons charged with burglary, auto theft, sex crimes and narcotics, an equal or greater proportion of those in custody were *not* convicted as of those on bail. Secondly, the authors admitted that:

> One of the primary reasons for this difference is the much higher proportion of *nol prosses* in the bail cases. Only ten out of 417 jail case indictments were *nol prossed*, or 2.4 per cent, whereas there were 160 *nol prosses* in bail cases, or 30.2 per cent of all bail indictments.... While jail cases came to trial in about a month after preliminary hearing, the time required to bring a bail case to trial was nine months. Some *nol prosses*, therefore, may simply

mean that the failure to provide a speedy trial has resulted in the loss of valuable evidence.

(Foote et al, 1954, p.1052)

The important influence upon the statistics of the large number of bail cases which were not proceeded with before trial is usually overlooked by those who cite these research findings, and if these *nol prosse* cases are eliminated from the initial analysis, it is found that only 25 per cent of bail defendants who went to trial were not convicted, while jail defendants were not convicted in 16.5 per cent of the cases.

In 1956 a study was made of 3,223 felony cases heard in New York City courts (Roberts and Palermo, 1958). It was found that 20 per cent of the defendants in custody were acquitted, compared to 31 per cent of those on bail; the authors, however, felt justified in drawing only tentative conclusions from these statistics:

These figures tend to support the propositions advanced earlier that jail in itself is likely to produce a guilty plea and that incarceration impairs a defendant's ability to defend himself. But the differences are not large and could be due in some measure to the fact that magistrates often set higher bail and thus keep the defendant in jail, in cases where they realize that the weight of evidence is against him.

(Roberts & Palermo, 1958, p.727)

Friedland's study of the 6,000 cases heard by the Toronto magistrates' courts, in the six months following September, 1961, provides the most sophisticated analysis of this aspect of the problem (Friedland, 1965). His initial analysis of the acquittal rate in cases where there was a plea of not guilty, showed that (a) in summary offences, 43 per cent of those on bail and 33 per cent of those in custody were acquitted; (b) in indictable offences, 55 per cent of those on bail and 43 per cent of those in custody were acquitted; and (c) in all offences, 47 per cent of those on bail and 41 per cent of those in custody were acquitted.

Friedland recognized that although the above figures are consistent with the theory that custody adversely affects the outcome of the trial, many of the factors which have a bearing on whether an accused remains in custody, such as the strength of the Crown's case and the accused's previous criminal record, also have a bearing on the outcome of the trial. Two further analyses were therefore carried out, to investigate factors which might influence the difference between bail and custody cases. When the analysis was restricted to cases where bail was initially set at $500, 55 per cent of those persons who were released on this bail were acquitted, compared to 39 per cent of those who were in custody because they were unable to raise this amount[1]. A second analysis, according to the accused's previous criminal record, showed that of all those with such a record, 61 per cent of those on bail and 38 per cent of those in custody were acquitted.

The present research into the practice of four English courts was on a much smaller scale than those projects in the United States and Canada, and this was a particular handicap in analysing possible differences within the small group of persons acquitted.

In the basic sample of 203 persons remanded in the urban court, only 4 per cent of those who were tried summarily were found not guilty: five of these six persons had been on bail all the time before trial, and the sixth had been part of the time on bail and part in custody. Similarly, at the rural courts, only 5 per cent of those tried summarily were found not guilty: only one of the seven persons had been in custody all the time, with a further two in custody for part of the time on remand before trial.

The acquittal rate of the cases which were committed for trial to a higher court was greater than that of those tried in the magistrates' court. In the cases from the urban court, 18 per cent of those committed in custody were acquitted, compared to 27 per cent of those on bail; but this still meant that exactly 50 per cent of the total acquitted had been in custody before trial. In the cases from the rural courts, 8 per cent of those committed for trial in custody were acquitted, compared to 18 per cent of those on bail; this meant that only 30 per cent of the total acquitted had been in custody. These figures, therefore, do appear to provide slight confirmation of the association that has been found in other countries. However, it was possible to carry out a small analysis which took into account the *plea* at trial, and this revealed a possibly very important intervening factor.

Information about the plea was available for those cases which were committed for trial by the urban court. This showed that 39 per cent of those committed in custody pleaded not guilty, of whom 46 per cent were acquitted; on the other hand, as many as 64 per cent of those committed on bail pleaded not guilty, of whom only 43 per cent were acquitted. Thus, from these figures, when the plea was taken into account the differential acquittal rate of bail and custody cases not only disappeared but moved slightly in the other direction. Nevertheless, despite this possible explanation, it could be argued by those who are convinced of the detrimental effect of a remand in custody upon the outcome of the trial that this same effect is equally operative at the earlier stage of influencing the plea of

1. This analysis implicitly took no account of cases in which the magistrate deliberately set bail at a level which they believed to be high enough to keep the defendant in custody; see the comments of Foote et al (1954, p. 1054): 'If the magistrates are sufficiently sagacious to impose bail predominantly upon those who are in fact guilty, and are lenient with those who are in fact not guilty, then to that extent the higher proportion among jail defendants of those adjudged guilty will *not* reflect any handicap from jail status.'

the accused, so that any comparison which controls this factor is likely to be controlling one of the main causal links between being remanded in custody and being subsequently found guilty.

Final judgement must be reserved on this aspect of the problem. It seems fairly well established that a greater proportion of persons remanded on bail are acquitted than of those remanded in custody. When account is taken of the plea of the accused at his trial, as in the Toronto study and in the present survey, this differential acquittal rate seems to decrease considerably or completely disappear. This may be simply pushing back the problem to discover why more persons in custody plead guilty than those on bail. On the other hand, the explanation of the higher conviction rate of those in custody may be that, when they are deciding about bail, the magistrates are influenced by the weight of the evidence against the accused, and the likelihood of his subsequent conviction. As Zander says, in the most recent and comprehensive examination of the problem in England : 'It may be that these figures merely indicate the skill of the courts in selecting for bail those who are not guilty. But this is mere guesswork. We do not know whether it is correct.' (Zander, 1967, p.27)

Custodial and non-custodial sentences

There is a great deal of evidence which shows that persons remanded in custody are much more likely to receive a custodial sentence than are persons released on bail before trial. This statistical evidence will be examined briefly, before consideration is given to some suggested explanations of this further possible effect of remands in custody upon the outcome of the trial.

The Philadelphia study, carried out by the University of Pennsylvania, showed that 22 per cent of those on bail who were convicted received a prison sentence, compared to 59 per cent of those who had been in custody before trial (Foote et al, 1954, p.1053). This difference in the relative proportions sentenced to imprisonment still existed when the various offence groups were considered separately: more offenders in custody were sentenced to imprisonment on conviction, whatever the offence.

In the larger scale study of the administration of bail in New York City (Roberts & Palermo, 1956), it was found that 84 per cent of the convicted defendants appearing in custody were sentenced to a penal institution, compared to only 45 per cent of those appearing on bail.

Friedland found that in Toronto 41 per cent of all offenders in custody before trial were sentenced to imprisonment, compared to only 13 per cent of those on bail; when only indictable offences were considered, 61 per cent of those in custody were subsequently imprisoned, compared to 15 per cent of those on bail (Friedland,

1965, p.120). As in his analysis of the acquittal rate, an attempt was made to 'equalize' the cases, by comparing all the offences in which bail was initially set at $500 : the results confirmed the previous findings, as 40 per cent of those persons in custody were imprisoned, compared to 18 per cent of those on bail.

The most detailed examination of the relationship between pretrial detention and sentence is an analysis of 732 felony cases in New York City, by Anne Rankin (1964). Sixty-four per cent of the 358 offenders who were in custody before trial were sentenced to imprisonment, compared to only 17 per cent of the 374 who had been remanded on bail. An attempt was made to see whether this large difference could be explained away by the different circumstances of the bail and custody cases, with regard to any of five selected factors, viz. previous criminal record, bail amount, private or assigned counsel, family integration and employment stability. The results of this complicated procedure suggested that none of these factors, individually or in combination, was responsible for the large proportion of custody cases sentenced to imprisonment. For example, in the analysis of the effect of previous criminal record, it was found that 59 per cent of the first offenders who were in custody were sentenced to imprisonment, compared to only 10 per cent of the first offenders who were on bail, and, conversely, 81 per cent of those with previous records who were in custody were sentenced to imprisonment compared to 36 per cent of those who were on bail.

Several reasons for this apparently well-attested relationship between remands in custody and a subsequent sentence of imprisonment have been suggested by the research workers in the United States. The two main suggestions are that, in the first place, a defendant remanded in custody is more likely to lose his job and consequently will not be considered as favourably for probation, and, in the second place, that his appearance in court and in the custody of the police or prison officers is likely to prejudice the magistrates against him, when deciding upon the appropriate sentence.

For example, the authors of the Philadelphia study drew the following conclusions :

> A number of factors might contribute to this difference. If the jail defendant had a job when he was arrested, he will have lost it and probably cannot get it back, whereas the defendant who is on bail can usually make the argument that probation will enable him to continue working on a job he holds. . . . And the fact that the jail defendant has been isolated in jail and cannot help himself, may also mean that the jail defendant is much less likely to have character witnesses who will appear to urge mitigation of penalty. Such circumstances help explain the inference raised by

> these statistics that, unconsciously or not, jail status prejudices the courts as to the treatment they prescribe.
>
> (Foote et al, 1954, p. 1053)

A more detailed comment is made by Patricia Wald in the Foreword to the New York study of Anne Rankin:

> A criminal sentence is generally thought to be an alloy of many factors: the nature and circumstances of the crime, the accused's plea, the evidence at trial, the skill of defence counsel, the accused's personality, demeanour, past record and rehabilitative prospects, the deterrent effects of his sentence on others, and the judge's own views on sentencing. *This study suggests that we can no longer disregard the impact of prior detention, as well, on the sentencing process* [italics added] . . . The present study is consistent with the hypothesis that detention erodes the rehabilitative prospects of an accused. A breadwinner and family man is more likely than a drifter to be freed on bail before trial. Logically, he should also be a better probation risk after conviction. But prior detention may stultify these prospects; the study at least raises the suspicion that a good rehabilitative risk in terms of community adjustment at the time of arrest loses much of his advantage over the poor risk defendant if he has been detained in the interim. Moreover, since imprisonment has traditionally been held by many to be an important factor in the rate of recidivism among convicted criminals, is there any reason to think the same experience will be less detrimental when it precedes conviction?
>
> (Wald, 1964, p. 635)

The small amount of evidence from England seems to show a very similar picture. The Home Office Research Unit (1960) found that 40 per cent of persons convicted after being committed for trial on bail were given a custodial sentence, compared to 78 per cent of those who had been committed for trial in custody[1]; and, in cases tried summarily, 14 per cent of those remanded on bail were given a custodial sentence, compared to 39 per cent of those in custody[2].

In our urban court sample, 56 per cent of those committed for trial on bail were given a custodial sentence, compared to 74 per cent of those committed in custody; and, in summary cases, 12 per cent of those remanded on bail were given a custodial sentence, compared to 64 per cent of those in custody.

In the sample from the rural courts, 47 per cent of those committed for trial on bail were given a custodial sentence, compared to 85 per cent of those committed in custody; and, in summary cases, 12 per cent of those on bail, but 62 per cent of those in custody were

1. Home Office Research Unit, *Time Spent Awaiting Trial,* (1960) Table 8, p. 11.
2. *Op. cit.* Table 28, p. 28.

given a custodial sentence. In both the urban and rural cases the proportion of offenders tried summarily who received a custodial sentence was very much greater than that found by the Home Office.

It was decided to make an analysis of the whole sample, in order to test the American findings that neither the offence nor the offender's previous criminal record is responsible for the difference in the proportion of custodial sentences.

Although there was a considerable range in the proportion who received custodial sentences, from 28 per cent of Group A who were tried summarily, to 75 per cent of Group A who were committed for trial, yet in each offence group a much larger proportion of those remanded in custody always received a custodial sentence. This was particularly noticeable in the cases which were tried summarily, where there was never less than a 50 per cent difference in the proportions.

TABLE 6

Percentage of offenders given a custodial sentence, according to previous criminal record and remand on bail or in custody.

	TOTAL		BAIL		CUSTODY	
	Custodial sentence		Custodial sentence		Custodial sentence	
	%	(no.)	%	(no.)	%	(no.)
*Committed for trial**						
No previous convictions	43·5	(10)	47·4	(9)	25·0	(1)
1 ∠ 3 p.cons.	68·0	(17)	61·5	(8)	75·0	(9)
3 or more p.cons.	76·0	(44)	42·8	(6)	84·0	(38)
TOTAL	67·0	(71)	50·0	(23)	80·0	(48)
*Tried summarily**						
No previous convictions	13·3	(11)	7·4	(4)	28·0	(1)
1 ∠ 3 p.cons.	30·0	(18)	7·4	(2)	55·2	(16)
3 or more p.cons.	69·6	(69)	31·2	(5)	77·0	(64)
TOTAL	41·2	(98)	10·9	(11)	63.5	(87)

* Cases in *Committed for trial* are divided into bail and custody according to the decision after committal for trail; those in *Tried summarily* include only those who spent *all* their remands *either* on bail *or* in custody.

The effect of controlling the influence of the offenders' previous criminal record (Table 6) was to reduce the gap between the proportions on bail and in custody who received custodial sentences; in fact, in the case of those persons with no previous convictions who were tried at a higher court, 47 per cent of those on bail were given a custodial sentence compared to only 25 per cent of those in custody.

In cases committed for trial, it was only for offenders who had a record of three or more previous convictions that the difference in sentence was as great as for all cases; in cases tried summarily, offenders with previous convictions were differentiated according to whether they were on bail or in custody, but the difference was very much reduced for persons with no previous convictions. It will be seen that the criminal record had an important influence on the granting of bail; in this sample, two-thirds of first offenders and persons with less than three previous convictions were committed for trial on bail, compared to less than a quarter of those with three or more convictions; of persons tried summarily, six out of ten first offenders and persons with less than three previous convictions were remanded on bail, compared to only one out of six of those with three or more convictions. It may well be the case that, on the comparatively rare occasions when magistrates granted bail to a person with a long criminal record, there were some exceptionally mitigating factors which not only influenced them in this decision but also influenced the later sentencing decision.

In *Time Spent Awaiting Trial* the Home Office Research Unit (1960) stated, in a single sentence, their interpretation of the discrepancy between the proportions remanded on bail and in custody who are given a custodial sentence—'The difference no doubt reflects the policy of the magistrates in selecting persons for bail' (p.11). The arguments which have been put forward to explain this difference as a direct result of custodial remands do not seem to be very plausible. The loss of a job, as a direct consequence of being remanded in custody, is not likely to be a great handicap in prejudicing a convicted offender's chance of probation, if his previous work record is good; and if, when arrested, he is in the kind of regular employment which might influence a subsequent decision in favour of a probation order, he is much more likely to be granted bail before trial. Secondly, the prejudice created by appearing in court in custody could only discriminate in favour of persons on bail in magistrates' courts in England, as at Quarter Sessions and Assizes all the accused appear in the same dock, and there is usually no obvious indication to the court whether a man appears in custody or on bail; because the difference in the proportion receiving custodial sentences obtains for higher courts as well as for lower, this argument loses much of its validity.

The authors of the Philadelphia study admit the possibility of other unknown variables, in the course of their argument which leads towards the virtually foregone conclusion:

> There are other variables, however, which cannot be resolved.... The fact that some magistrates penalize what they regard as aggravated circumstances by setting higher bail may concentrate the aggravated cases in jail and thus partially explain the more severe punishment of the guilty offenders in the jail group. One distinction between the jail group and the bail group is the comparatively lower economic status of the former. This factor would also explain in part the different treatment of these two groups.... Des-

pite these unmeasureable variables, however, the contrast in comparative dispositions was so striking that it is reasonable to conclude that jail status had a good deal to do with it.

(Foote et al, 1954, p. 1054.)

After a comprehensive survey of the existing research evidence, Zander likewise rejects the explanation which attributes the difference to the selective policy of magistrates, when initially deciding upon the granting of bail, and favours the explanation which attributes the difference to the fact of being in custody before trial (Zander, 1967, pp 36–7).

No interpretation can be conclusive; the nature of the available evidence does not allow this. Any interpretation of the apparent statistical correlations must be assessed in terms of *prima facie* plausibility and apparent probability. None of the suggested explanations of the way in which a remand in custody before trial is likely substantially to affect the chance of a subsequent custodial sentence appears either very plausible or very probable. It seems much more likely that when magistrates decide, in the first instance, to grant or to refuse bail they take into consideration very similar factors to those which will be taken into account in the sentencing decision. The analysis of the English urban and rural sample showed that when previous criminal record was taken into account much of the difference disappeared, in apparent contradiction to the evidence from America; only in the case of offenders with a long criminal record was the difference not reduced, and this could be due, in a similar way, to special factors which are likely to be present if such an offender is granted bail before trial.

4. THE DECISION-MAKING PROCESS OF THE COURTS

Certain important aspects of remands in custody could only be studied by direct observation of the decision-making process in magistrates' courts. The two main purposes of observation at the four English courts selected for study were (i) to examine the patterns of procedure in remand hearings, including an analysis of the amount and type of information available to the court when reaching its decision, and (ii) to observe more specifically the role of the police.

Observation at the urban court extended over a consecutive period of nine weeks, June-August, 1965, during which the court was attended each day, for six days a week. During this period a total of 128 remands before trial were observed[1].

Observation at the three rural courts necessarily extended for a longer period, in order to observe an adequate number of remands, as each court sat on only one day each week. Combining the periods of observation at all three courts, April-December, 1966, a total of 60 court sessions were attended and 43 remands before trial were observed[1].

This chapter will describe certain features of the decision-making process of the courts, and Chapter 5 will describe the role of the police in opposing bail.

Patterns of court procedure

In most respects, the decision which has to be made, when a person is remanded, is very much simpler than the sentencing decision. It is simpler partly because there are only three alternatives open to the court : the defendant must be either (a) remanded in custody, (b) remanded on bail in his own recognisance, or (c) remanded on bail with one or more sureties. However, observation of court practice showed that there were several 'routes' by which the final decision could be reached. It was possible to map these alternative routes, and thereby discover the most frequent ways in which persons at the observed courts were dealt with.

1. For further methodological details of the periods of observation, see the Appendix.

Cases could be divided initially into whether the police (or prosecution) or the defendant requested the adjournment. Figures 1 and 2 show diagrammatically the subsequent stages of cases initiated in each of these ways.

When the prosecution asked for a remand (Fig. 1), there were various intermediate stages at which different courses of action might be taken. In the first place, the police could either object to bail or not; if they did object to bail (stage 2), the defendant had then to decide whether or not to apply for bail, and if there was no such application (stage 4) almost invariably the defendant was remanded in custody; but if the defendant did apply for bail (stage 5) there was then a better chance of being eventually remanded on bail, with or without sureties. If, on the other hand, the police did *not* object to bail, they might ask for sureties (stage 7), in which case the magistrates had to decide whether or not they considered them to be necessary; but if the police did not press for sureties (stage 6), almost invariably the magistrates remanded the defendant on bail in his own recognisance alone.

When the defendant himself (or his solicitor) requested an adjournment (Fig. 2), this was almost always accompanied by an application for bail. The police could still object to bail, but if there were no police objections (stage C) it had simply to be decided whether or not any sureties were necessary (stages D and E).

It is clear, from the discussion so far, that there were many different patterns of procedure in the observed cases, but it was felt that unless close attention was paid to these differences of procedure it would not be possible to draw useful conclusions from the observed evidence. It was found necessary to distinguish eight different ways in which persons were remanded, as follows:

Pattern–A Prosecution requests remand; no police objections to bail in the defendant's own recognisance.
[Fig. 1: stages 1, 3 and 6]

Pattern–B: Prosecution requests remand; no police objections to bail, but a request for sureties.
[Fig. 1: stages 1, 3 and 7]

Pattern–C: Prosecution requests remand; police object to bail; defendant does not apply for bail.
[Fig. 1: stages 1, 2 and 4]

Pattern–D: Prosecution requests remand; police object to bail; defendant (not legally represented) asks for bail.
[Fig. 1: stages 1, 2 and 5]

Pattern–E: Prosecution requests remand; police object to bail; Defence Solicitor asks for bail for his client.
[Fig. 1: stages 1, 2 and 5]

FIGURE 1 *Diagrammatic scheme of decision patterns in remand hearings.*
A. Prosecution requests remand.

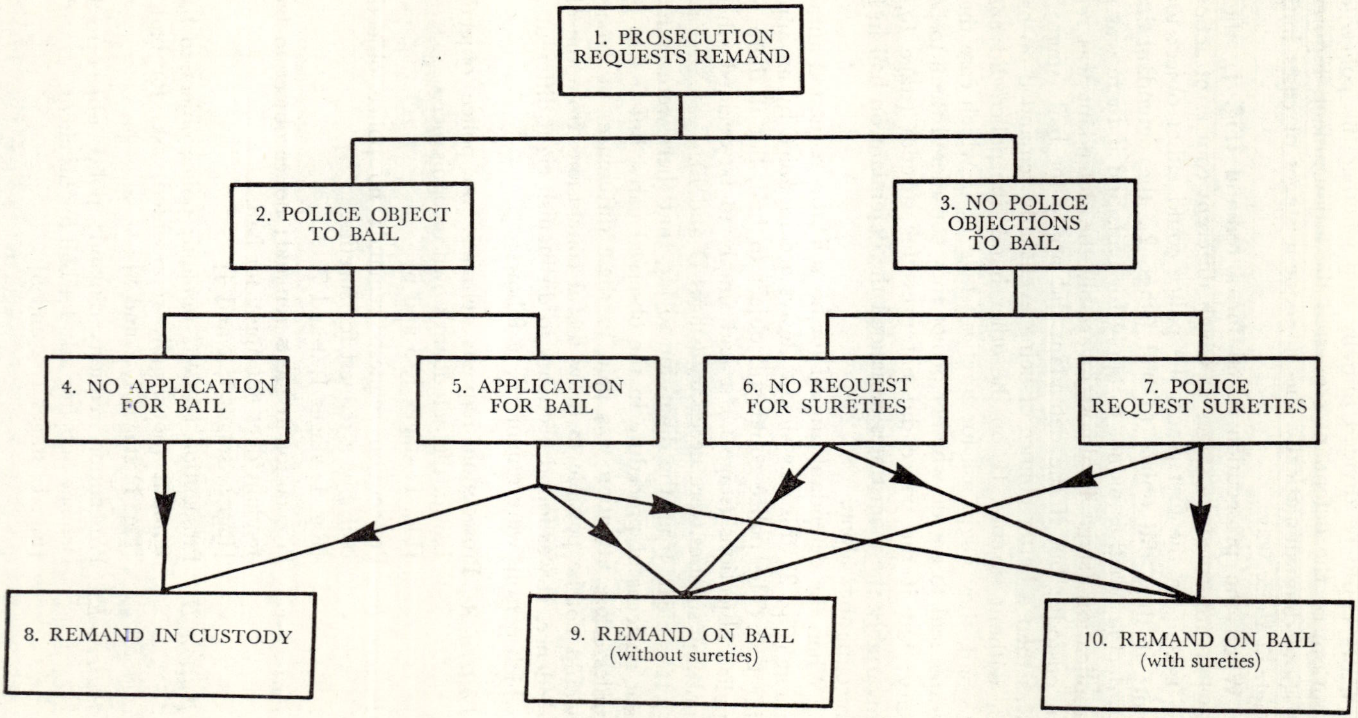

FIGURE 2 *Diagrammatic scheme of decision patterns in remand hearings. B. Defence requests adjournment.*

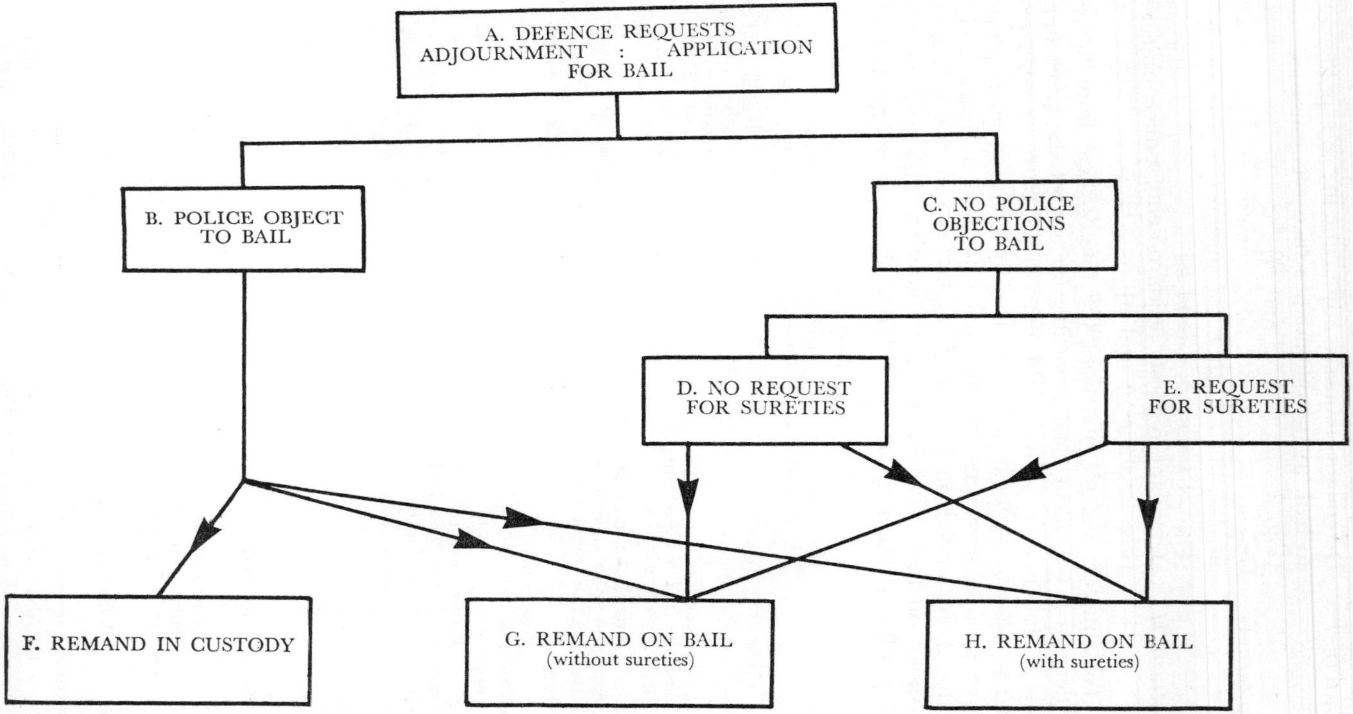

Pattern–F: Defendant requests adjournment; no police objections to bail, in the defendant's own recognisance. [Fig. 2: stages A, C and D]

Pattern–G: Defendant requests adjournment; no police objections to bail, but a request for sureties. [Fig. 2: stages A, C and E]

Pattern–H: Defendant requests adjournment; police object to bail. [Fig. 2: stages A and B]

To complete the classification, the magistrates' final decision was added; as it was theoretically possible for any of the three final decisions to follow any of the eight procedural patterns, this possibility had to be schematically provided for, by dividing each pattern into three groups, according to the final outcome: 1. remanded in custody; 2. remanded on bail, in defendant's own recognisance; 3. remanded on bail, with one or more sureties. This created a total of 24 possible decision patterns. Table 7 shows how the 171 observed

TABLE 7

A classification of decision patterns in remand hearings: distribution of the observed cases.

Decision Pattern	1. Remand in Custody	2. Bail without Sureties	3. Bail with Sureties	TOTAL no.	(%)
A: Prosecution requests remand; no police objections to bail, without sureties.	—	33	1	34	(19·9)
B: Prosecution requests remand; no police objections to bail, but a request for sureties.	1	1	25	27	(15·8)
C: Prosecution requests remand; police object to bail; no application for bail.	44	—	—	44	(25·7)
D: Prosecution requests remand; police object to bail; defendant applies for bail.	20	1	1	22	(12·9)
E: Prosecution requests remand; police object to bail; Defence Solicitor applies for bail.	21	—	5	26	(15·2)
F: Defendant requests adjournment; no police objections to bail, without sureties.	—	15	—	15	(8·8)
G: Defendant requests adjournment; no police objections to bail, but request sureties.	—	1	—	1	(0·6)
H: Defendant requests adjournment; police object to bail.	2	—	—	2	(1·2)
GRAND TOTAL:	88	51	32	171	
(%)	(51·5)	(29·8)	(18·7)	(100·0)	

cases were distributed among the various possible patterns; three-quarters (128) of the cases were at the urban court, and one quarter (43) at the rural courts.

Half of all cases resulted in remands in custody; almost 30 per cent in remands on bail, in the defendant's own recognisance; and nearly one-fifth in remands on bail with sureties. Over 55 per cent of the urban cases were remands in custody, compared to only 40 per cent of the rural; of those persons remanded on bail, 77 per cent at the rural courts were released in their own recognisances, compared to only 54 per cent of those at the urban court.

A summary of the main points arising from a closer analysis of this information can be divided into three sections: (a) remands in custody, (b) remands on bail, and (c) police recommendations.

(*a*) *Remands in custody*. In exactly half of the cases which resulted in remands in custody, the defendant (or, in 5 of the 44 cases, his solicitor) did not apply for bail (Pattern C1). This was a slightly more common occurrence at the urban court, where 52 per cent of those remanded in custody did not apply for bail, compared to 41 per cent at the rural courts.

In 20 cases (23 per cent of those remanded in custody), the defendant himself made an unsuccessful application for bail, in the face of police objections (Pattern D1); only two other such applications were successful.

In 21 cases (24 per cent), the defendant's solicitor made an unsuccesful application for bail (Pattern E1); five other such applications were successful, in all of which the defendant was remanded on bail with sureties.

In two cases, the defendant was remanded in custody after having requested the adjournment himself, but with the police objecting to bail (Pattern H1). There was only one instance in which a person was remanded in custody when there were no police objections to bail (Pattern B1); in this instance, although the offence had been committed on bail, the police were prepared to accept his father as surety, but the magistrates decided not to take the risk and remanded him in custody

(*b*) *Remands on bail*. In only seven of the ninety-four cases, in which bail was granted by the magistrates, had the police objected to bail; in all but one of these seven cases the magistrates asked for sureties from the defendant, and in five of them the defendant was legally represented.

In 32 cases (a third of those granted bail) bail was conditional upon suitable sureties being provided; twenty-one of these were instances where the police did not object to bail *per se* but requested sureties (Pattern B3); six were those cases mentioned above, in which the police had objected to bail, but the magistrates had decided to grant bail with sureties; thus, there was only the one remaining case in which the magistrates requested sureties from the defendant, entirely on their own initiative (Pattern A3). There were just two cases in which the defendant was released in his own recognisance, despite the fact that the police had requested sureties.

In all but two of the eighteen cases, in which the defendant had asked for the adjournment, bail was granted in his own recognisance; in the two exceptions (both of which were, in fact, legally represented) the police successfully opposed bail (Pattern H1).

(*c*) *Police recommendations.* The overall picture which emerges from Table 7 is one of only a small number of cases in which the final decision of the magistrates went against the implicit or explicit recommendations of the police, not only with regard to recommendations whether the remand should be on bail or in custody, but even with regard to whether or not bail should be granted with sureties. In the total number of 171 remand decisions, only eleven (6 per cent) were not in complete accord with police recommendations: in two of these instances the magistrates took a firmer line than the police by, in one case, requesting a surety when the police had no objection to release in the defendant's own recognisance, and, in the other case, by remanding a person in custody when the police had no objection to bail, providing that suitable sureties were forthcoming; but in the remaining nine decisions, the magistrates were more 'lenient' than the police, either by releasing on bail a person for whom the police had objected to bail (7 cases), or by releasing on bail, in his own recognisance, a person for whom the police had requested the provision of sureties (2 cases).

To summarize the extent to which police recommendations were followed: the police requested a remand in custody in ninety-four cases, and it was granted in eighty-seven cases (93 per cent); they requested release on bail in the defendant's own recognisance in forty-nine cases, and it was granted in forty-eight cases (98 per cent); and finally, the police requested release on bail with sureties in twenty-eight cases, and it was granted in twenty-five cases (90 per cent).

The final aspect of court procedure which was observed, providing a link with the analysis, which follows, of the type of information available to the court, was an examination of the way in which information was provided to the court, by whom and at what stage in the proceedings.

It was found that in forty-eight cases (28 per cent) no information at all was provided, and this included as many as a third of those cases in which the person was remanded in custody, after the police had objected to bail and he had not applied for bail (Pattern C1).

In sixty-seven cases (39 per cent), the only information was provided by the Prosecuting Solicitor or Police Inspector, when initially applying for a remand; this was the common pattern in two-thirds of the cases in which the police had no objections to bail (Patterns

A and B), and also in the remaining two-thirds of the cases in Pattern C1. where the defendant did not apply for bail.

C.I.D. officers were called to give evidence and relevant information in thirty-eight cases (22 per cent); all but four of these cases were those in which the defendant had applied for bail, to which the police had objections (Patterns D and E). Information was provided by the defendant or his solicitor in the remaining eighteen cases (11 per cent).

Summarizing the various relationships between the patterns of court procedure and the provision of information by the C.I.D: it was found that in less than one in ten of the remands in custody, where the defendant did not apply for bail (Pattern C1), was a C.I.D. officer called to state the reasons for the police request for a remand in custody; in over three-quarters of the cases where the defendant (or his solicitor) did apply for bail, and where there were police objections (Patterns D and E) a C.I.D. officer was called to give evidence of the police objections to bail, and he was invariably cross-examined by the Defence Solicitor; and, finally, in only one of the 77 cases where bail was granted without any police objections (Patterns A, B, F and G) was a C.I.D. officer called to give evidence of arrest or to provide information to the court about the reliability of the defendant; in fact, in thirty-one of these cases (42 per cent) no information whatsoever was provided for the court, except that the police had no objection to bail.

Discretion, information and objectives

Before the new provisions of the Criminal Justice Act, 1967, magistrates had an unfettered discretion to grant or refuse bail to a person charged with any indictable offence (except treason). One of the aims of the observation of decision-making in the courts was to try to examine the reality and meaning of 'discretion' in this particular context.

A recent trend in the development of criminology in this country has been the increasing attention paid to problems of decision-making in the penal system. Leslie T. Wilkins can, perhaps, claim much of the credit for focusing attention on this particular aspect[1], and in his book *Social Deviance* (1964) he put forward a simplified definition of 'rationality', which can be applied to the decision-making of the magistrates.

The three essential elements of this definition of rationality are, in Wilkins' terminology: (i) information, (ii) room for manoeuvre (possible decisions), and (iii) purpose or 'pay-off'. He explained the important relationship between these three elements:

1. See the early discussion in H. Mannheim and L. T. Wilkins, *Prediction Methods in Relation to Borstal Training*, (London, 1955), pp. 216–17.

> Clearly, if we do not know what we wish to achieve there is no meaning in any information; similarly, if we can make only one decision (a rare situation) there is no point in discussing the other two dimensions; again, if no information can be available, one cannot discuss rationality. A rational decision may, it seems, be defined as the decision which, having regard to the information available, maximises the likelihood of obtaining the purpose we wish to acheive or minimises our probability of loss.
>
> (Wilkins, 1964, p. 18)

Wilkins maintains that a decision, which is made on the basis of no information whatsoever, can be assessed either in ethical terms as right or wrong, or alternatively in terms of achieving its objective as effective or ineffective, but it cannot be criticized as irrational without there being some information as a criterion of possible rationality:

> Immediately information becomes available, it becomes possible to put forward arguments in favour of some decisions rather than others, and, indeed, the number of rational decisions will tend to diminish as information increases. . . . In the sense in which information is discussed in the argument here, it is information relevant to the *objective* . . . If the objectives are ambiguous, the relationship between my decision and the information cannot be tied down. Thus there is an interdependence between decisions, information and objectives (Wilkins, 1964, pp. 19–20)

Little empirical research has so far been carried out in England to test these theories of decision-making, as applicable to magistrates' courts. However, a current enquiry into the sentencing policy and practice of magistrates' courts, towards motoring offenders, is being carried out by Dr. Roger Hood and Dr. Terence Willett, and this research includes a sophisticated analysis of the decision-making process in the thirty-two magistrates' courts being studied (Hood, 1966). Some of the relevant factors being examined include the magistrates' views on the aims which particular sentences are intended to achieve, and court practices affecting the information made known to the bench.

The Sentencing Research Project, being carried out at the Centre of Criminology, University of Toronto, under the direction of Professor John Hogarth, also incorporates a similar theoretical framework for part of its analysis of decision-making of Canadian magistrates. Like the research of Hood and Willett, the focus of the Toronto research is upon the total setting in which the sentencing decision is reached, but one of the hypotheses to be tested states:

> That sentences imposed by magistrates are consistent with (a) the information available to the court, (b) the magistrates' perception

of that information, and (c) the express reason or purpose of the sentence imposed.

(Hogarth, 1967a, p. 88)

Hogarth has said that the manner in which information is used by the court is more likely to influence the sentencing decision than is merely the quantity or quality of the information, and it is only when information is available that a court's discretion can be exercised with proper responsibility:

> Real discretion can only be exercised in full awareness of pertinent information. Decision-making in ignorance of pertinent information is not the exercise of discretion, it is pure speculation. In any event, factual questions do not admit of discretion. Discretion only enters into the decision-making phase at the level of making value judgements in the light of the best information available.
>
> (Hogarth, 1967b, pp. 13–14.)

It was possible to examine the applicability of some of these concepts to the remand decisions which were studied during the periods of court observation.

In the previous section of this chapter, it was noted that in 28 per cent of all remand decisions no information whatsoever was provided to the court, about the person being remanded or the offence with which he was charged. All but one of these 48 decisions, where there was no information, occurred in two groups of cases, and it is the evidence from these groups in particular which raises serious questions as to the reality and meaning of the magistrates' discretion in this context.

The first group included all those where there were no police objections to bail; there were 77 cases in this group, which constituted 45 per cent of the total number. In thirty-two of these cases (42 per cent), no information at all was provided for the magistrates, and in the remaining forty-five cases usually the only kind of information provided by the Prosecuting Solicitor or Police Inspector, applying for the remand, concerned the details of arrest or a brief statement about the alleged offence.

Table 8 details the scope of information provided in this first group of cases. In twelve of the cases at the urban court, the only information provided by the police was that the defendant admitted the offence; thus, in over 80 per cent of the urban cases there was no information about the arrest or the nature of the alleged offence. Only twelve cases out of the seventy-seven included any details about the defendant's 'community ties'[1], and in the majority of these it was usually just a single detail, about his job or his family.

1. This is a short-hand phrase, used in the American literature, which refers to several aspects of a person's social circumstances, e.g. employment, residence in area, marital status etc.

It seems that the only conclusion to be drawn from these observations is that, when the police did not object to bail, the magistrates apparently accepted on trust the defendant's reliability, as assessed by the police; in less than a fifth of the cases was any information provided about the defendant's background, which would have been supportive evidence for the judgement of the police.

TABLE 8

Information provided in cases where there were no police objections to bail (Patterns A,B,F and G)

Nature of information	TOTAL no.	(%)*	Urban Court no.	(%)*	Rural Courts no.	(%)*
No information	32	(41·5)	23	(44·3)	9	(36·0)
Details of arrest	18	(23·4)	6	(11·5)	12	(48·0)
Details of offence	16	(20·8)	4	(7·7)	12	(48·0)
Admits offence	14	(18·2)	14	(26·9)	—	—
Criminal record	3	(3·9)	3	(5·8)	—	—
Community ties	12	(15·6)	7	(13·5)	5	(20·0)
Will appear for trial	3	(3·9)	3	(5·8)	—	—
(n =)	(77)		(52)		(25)	

* The percentages in this and the next three tables add up to more than 100 per cent, because some cases had more than one item of information.

The second group of cases, where there was a dearth of information, was that of those where the defendant did not make any application for bail. There were forty-four cases in this group, one-quarter of the total (29 per cent of the urban, 16 per cent of the rural cases), and there was no information in fifteen cases. In the remaining two-thirds of this group, details of arrest were given in sixteen cases; a brief item about some aspect of the defendant's family or employment was given in twelve cases, but these constituted only a quarter of a group of whom all were remanded in custody. Table 9 shows the frequency with which particular items of information were mentioned.

TABLE 9

Information provided in cases where the defendant did not apply for bail (Pattern C)

Nature of information	TOTAL no.	(%)	Urban Court no.	(%)	Rural Courts no.	(%)
No information	15	(34·1)	14	(37·8)	1	(14·3)
Details of arrest	16	(36·4)	12	(32·4)	4	(57·2)
Details of offence	10	(22·7)	7	(18·9)	3	(42·8)
Admits offence	8	(18·2)	7	(18·9)	1	(14·3)
Criminal record	4	(9·1)	4	(10·8)	—	—
Community ties	12	(27·3)	8	(21·6)	4	(57·2)
Mental history	1	(2·3)	1	(2·7)	—	—
(n =)	(44)		(37)		(7)	

Some illustrative detail of the usual procedure in these cases might help to set these statistics in a more real context.

The practice at the urban court, after the Prosecuting Solicitor had asked for a remand in custody, was for the Chairman of the Magistrates to ask the defendant:

'You have heard the application—have you anything to say?' The answer to this question was, invariably, simply—'No, sir.'

When the defendant was represented, his solicitor volunteered that he did not wish to apply for bail on behalf of his client. In only two cases was the defendant *not* asked if he had anything to say. Finally, in only two cases was it actually spelled out again by the Chairman that the 'application' involved being detained in custody.

The practice was slightly different at the rural courts. Here it was the Clerk to the Justices who always put the question to the defendant, and put it in a more explicit way:

> 'Have you any objection to being remanded in custody?' *or* 'Do you wish to apply for bail?'

Despite the more explicit nature of the question, the answer was equally invariably—'No, sir.'

When the liberty of the individual is involved, in decisions of this kind, there would seem to be strong grounds for requiring a much more positive exercise of discretion, and the discretion of magistrates could properly be seen as extending to include a more rigorous inquiry into why a defendant is not applying for bail, or into the possibility of a solicitor being briefed on his behalf.

The only kind of remand decision for which information was regularly provided was that in which the police had objections to an application for bail made by the defendant or his solicitor. In other words, information was mainly provided where there was an 'adversary' element involved, which inevitably meant that the information was more or less selective, depending on who was presenting it to the court.

This confirms a trend that was observed: it has already been seen that, where the police did not object to bail, a minimum amount of information (if any) was provided; that when the police objected to bail, even though the defendant might not subsequently make any application, a little more information was provided; now it will be seen that where the defendant did apply for bail (against police objections), much more information was provided, and that where he was legally represented the maximum amount of information was presented to the magistrates.

There were twenty-two cases in which the defendant himself applied for bail, with police objections. In only one of these cases was no information provided. However, in sixteen of the remaining cases all the information was provided by the prosecution; at the rural courts it was always given by the Prosecuting Solicitor or Police Inspector, but in thirteen out of the fourteen urban cases it was given by a C.I.D. officer called to the witness box. Not surprisingly the source of the information affected its nature, and Table 10 shows that much of it was identical to the usual reasons for police objections to bail (see Chapter 5). Five of the eleven cases, where there was information about a defendant's 'community ties', were those in which some of the information was presented on behalf of the defendant, rather than from the police or prosecution.

TABLE 10

Information provided in cases where the defendant applied for bail, and the police had objections (Pattern D)

Nature of information	TOTAL no.	(%)	Urban Court no.	(%)	Rural Courts no.	(%)
No information	1	(4·5)	1	(5·9)	–	—
Details of arrest, and/or offence	19	(86·4)	14	(82·4)	5	(100·0)
Admits offence	4	(18·2)	4	(23·5)	–	—
Criminal record	13	(59·1)	9	(53·0)	4	(80·0)
Police inquiries	15	(68·2)	13	(76·5)	2	(40·0)
Serious offence	4	(18·2)	2	(11·8)	2	(40·0)
Threats to witnesses	1	(4·5)	1	(5·9)	–	—
Community ties	11	(50·0)	7	(41·2)	4	(80·0)
[n =]	[22]		[17]		[5]	

Finally, there were twenty-six cases in which a solicitor applied for bail on behalf of the defendant, with police objections. Some information was provided in all these cases, and if Table 11 is compared with Table 10 it can be seen that more information was provided in cases where the defendant was legally represented than where he applied for bail on his own behalf: on average, five different categories of information were provided in the former cases, compared to only three in the latter. Particularly significant is the fact

TABLE 11

Information provided in cases where the Defence Solicitor applied for bail, and the police had objections (Pattern E)

Nature of information	TOTAL no.	(%)	Urban Court no.	(%)	Rural Courts no.	(%)
Details of arrest, and/or offence	26	(100·0)	20	(100·0)	6	(100·0)
Admits offence	5	(19·2)	5	(25·0)	—	—
Criminal record	19	(73·1)	14	(70·0)	5	(83·4)
Police inquiries	15	(57·7)	12	(60·0)	3	(50·0)
Serious offence	10	(38·5)	10	(50·0)	—	—
Threats to witnesses	8	(30·8)	8	(40·0)	—	—
Community ties	26	(100·0)	20	(100·0)	6	(100·0)
Sureties available	16	(61·5)	13	(65·0)	3	(50·0)
Denies offence	6	(23·1)	5	(25·0)	1	(16·7)
[n =]	[26]		[20]		[6]	

that in all cases there was some information about the defendant's community ties, and in all but one case there were as many as three items of information in this category; practically all of it was provided by the solicitor, either directly in his application for bail, or indirectly through his cross-examination of the C.I.D. officer. On the other hand, the police or prosecution were the sole source of information with regard to details of arrest, offence, previous criminal record, further police enquiries and threats to witnesses.

This analysis of the amount of information provided for magistrates at remand hearings seems to confirm earlier doubts about the realities of the exercise of discretion in these circumstances. It was only in cases when either the defendant or his solicitor applied for bail, in the face of police opposition, that relatively comprehensive information was put before the court, and these cases constituted only slightly more than one-quarter of the total. When little or no information was provided, no meaning could properly be attached to the concept of discretion, and in such cases the decisions could not possibly satisfy Wilkins' criteria of 'rationality'. However, in the minority of cases where substantial information was provided, it is possible to consider the relationship between this information and the objectives of the decision, to test this particular criterion of rationality, in the light of Wilkins' definition of a rational decision as '... the decision which, having regard to the information available, maximises the likelihood of obtaining the purpose we wish to achieve or minimises our probability of loss' (Wilkins, 1964, p. 18). When the objectives are ambiguous, the relationship between the decision and the information must also be ambiguous; thus, if magistrates do not know or are uncertain about what they wish to achieve, the most comprehensive amount of information is of little value.

In order to present the argument here, it is necessary to anticipate some of the evidence which will be presented in the next chapter. From the results of an examination of the legal background of bail decisions (Bottomley, 1968), and an investigation of the main reasons for which police objected to bail at the observed courts (Chapter 5), it was possible to make certain tentative assumptions about the purposes and objectives which magistrates may have had in mind when considering the information available to them for their remand decisions, and to examine the extent to which the information could be related to these possible objectives.

Three possible objectives were identified:

(i) to ensure the defendant's appearance at his trial;
(ii) to prevent the repetition of the offence, or similar offences; and
(iii) to prevent the course of justice from being impeded, in other ways.

In each remand case, one or more of these objectives may have been uppermost in the minds of the magistrates, and although in a majority of cases little information of any kind was provided, yet in a minority of cases information was provided which could be relevant to some or all of these possible objectives.

Information of particular relevance to the objective of ensuring a defendant's appearance at trial would probably include details of his community ties, descriptions of the seriousness of the offence, and police evidence about the likelihood of his guilt, often based on an alleged admission by the accused himself. The amount of information of this kind was negligible in cases where there were no police objections to bail (Table 8) or where the defendant did not apply for bail (Table 9), but in a majority of cases where bail was applied for, against police objections, relevant information was provided (Tables 10 and 11).

The second possible objective was to prevent the repetition of offences; relevant information would probably include police details of the offence and arrest, and also the defendant's previous criminal record. Once again, in the vast majority of cases where there was an application for bail with opposition from the police, relevant information was provided, and, even in the remaining cases, police evidence of arrest and the nature of the alleged offences were the most frequent types of information provided.

The third possible objective was to prevent the course of justice from being impeded, and the main type of information relevant to this was evidence from the police about likely hampering of their further inquiries, including interference with witnesses. Not surprisingly, there was no information of this kind where the police did not object to bail, and neither was there any such information in cases where the defendant did not apply for bail; however, in two-thirds of the cases where the police objected to an application for bail, evidence of likely interference with the course of justice was given (Tables 10 and 11).

This brief discussion of the possible relationship between information and objectives is inevitably very speculative. Nevertheless, there seems to be a clear enough indication of the need for improvement in the provision of information, for without this *no* objective can be pursued in a rational way. In only twenty-six cases, out of the 171 which were observed, was comprehensive information presented to the magistrates either about the persons being remanded or about his alleged offence; these were all cases in which a solicitor applied for bail, on behalf of the defendant. In the remaining cases, not enough information was consistently provided to enable the magistrates to make a fully informed (i.e. 'rational') decision to achieve any particular objective which they might have had in mind.

Effectiveness and the use of sureties

It is very difficult to measure the success or effectiveness of the remand decisions made by the magistrates, even assuming that the possible objectives outlined in the previous section are generally valid. Persons who are remanded in custody necessarily appear for their trial, providing that they do not escape from prison or successfully apply for bail to a Judge in Chambers, and they are prevented in the meanwhile from committing further offences or directly interfering with the course of justice; but no one can be certain how many of these persons are *unnecessarily* remanded in custody, for the same results to be achieved. On the other hand, the effectiveness of decisions to release persons on bail can be measured to a limited extent, mainly by the proportion of persons on bail who fail to appear for trial.

During the periods of observation at the urban and rural courts there was no instance of a person being remanded on bail and subsequently failing to appear in court. In the representative sample of 416 cases from the same courts, there were two cases of bail-jumping, one from the urban court and one from the rural courts. On this evidence, the magistrates appeared to be successful at releasing on bail persons who will appear to take their trial.

It is virtually impossible to assess in any systematic way the success of the decisions, with regard to the commission of further offences on bail or the prevention of interference with police inquiries. The latter factor is the most unknown, and only the police themselves can have any idea of the extent to which persons on bail may have caused any interference; in only very rare instances can criminal acts of corruption be proved. Similarly, there is likely to be a considerable 'dark figure' of crimes committed by persons released on bail while awaiting trial. During observation, there were three instances, brought to the magistrates' notice by the police, of persons who had committed further offences after being released on bail, and all three cases were at the rural courts. Neither during observation at the urban court, nor from information from the files of the 203 urban remand cases in 1964, was there any recorded instance of a person committing further offences on bail.

If it is accepted that only one or two per cent of persons released on bail fail to appear for trial, how much can be attributed to the financial sanction of the bail recognisance and sureties? No regular information is published of the extent to which sureties are required by magistrates in England, nor of the amount of the bail recognisances. Some basic information was available from the sample of remand cases at the urban court, during 1964,[1] and more detailed

1. This information was not consistently available in the files of the rural cases, 1963–65, and so a similar analysis could not be carried out.

information from observation at the urban and rural court, 1965–1966.

Table 12 shows the proportion of cases at the urban court (1964) in which bail was granted in different amounts. In 55 per cent of the cases no sureties were required, and bail was granted simply in the defendant's own recognisance; in 80 per cent of such cases, the amount was less than £25, and in only two of the 41 cases was it £50 or more. In the remaining 45 per cent of the cases, where sureties were required, the total amount of the recognisances was calculated: in almost three-quarters of such cases the total amount was less than £100, and in only one instance was it over £200.

Table 12

Amounts of recognisances of persons granted bail, with or without sureties: Urban Court, 1964

Total amount of recognisances	All Cases %	Released on own recognisances %	Bail granted with sureties %
∠ £10	9·3	17·1	—
£10 ∠ £15	22·7	36·6	5·9
£15 ∠ £25	21·4	26·8	14·7
£25 ∠ £50	12·0	7·3	17·7
£50 ∠ £100	16·0	—	35·3
£100 ∠ £200	8·0	2·4	14·7
£200 and over	2·7	2·4	2·9
Not known	(8·0)	(7·3)	(8·8)
[n =]	[75]*	[41]	[34]

*Nine cases in which bail was granted are not included in this table, as no further details were known about them.

During the periods of observation at the urban and rural courts there were 83 remands on bail. Fifty-one of these remands (61 per cent) were granted without sureties; 90 per cent of them were in amounts of £25 or less, and in no case was the amount more than £50 (Table 13).

Table 13

Amounts of recognisances of persons granted bail without sureties: observed cases, 1965–66

Amount of recognisance	ALL CASES %	Urban Court %	Rural Courts %
£5	3·9	6·5	—
£10	23·5	12·9	40·0
£20	27·5	29·0	25·0
£25	35·3	41·9	25·0
£50	7·8	6·5	10·0
not known	(2·0)	(3·2)	—
[n =]	[51]	[31]	[20]

The remaining thirty-two cases (39 per cent) were granted bail with additional sureties; in 72 per cent of the cases, the total amount of the recognisances was £100 or less, and the highest were three cases each involving a total of £300 (Table 14).

In twenty-five of these thirty-two surety cases the police had not objected to bail provided that suitable sureties were forthcoming; six of the remaining cases were ones in which the magistrates had overruled police objections to bail but had requested sureties as an additional safeguard.

TABLE 14

Amounts of recognisances of persons granted bail with sureties: observed cases, 1965–66

Total amount of recognisances	ALL CASES	Urban Court	Rural Courts
	%	%	%
£20	12·5	11·5	16·7
£30	18·8	23·1	—
£40	12·5	7·7	33·3
£50	9·4	11·5	—
£100	18·8	23·1	—
£120	3·1	—	16·7
£150	9·4	11·5	—
£170	6·2	—	33·3
£300	9·4	11·5	—
[n =]	[32]	[26]	[6]

When comparing the practice of the urban and the rural courts, apart from the fact that more of the persons granted bail by the rural courts were not asked to provide sureties, there appeared to be very little difference in the amounts of recognisances which were required.

Although it was only a minority of bail cases in which sureties were requested, yet it is important to consider the mechanics of this particular process in order to discover whether a request for sureties was an empty formality or whether it was dealt with carefully by the magistrates, and was thus likely to prove a real guarantee to safeguard their decision.

In only a quarter of the cases were *two* sureties requested; the general practice was for just one to be required. Thus, in the 32 observed cases, there were 40 persons involved, acting as sureties. In more than half the cases, the person was known to be a close relative of the defendant, viz. father (12 cases), mother (7), or other close relative (5).

Twenty-two of the sureties were actually present in court during the remand hearing, and were sworn in at the witness box, when the magistrates had reached their decision. In eight cases, definite sureties were proposed by name, and it was stated that they would contact the police later that same day. In an additional seven cases, it was merely the continuation of previous bail with the same sureties, and no question of identification or reliability arose. Thus, in only three of the forty cases was there no mention of the proposed sureties, or of any mechanism for contacting them.

When the surety was present in court and immediately entered into his recognisance, additional information was often provided about his background, his knowledge of the defendant and the nature of his employment. This information was either volunteered by the defence or arose from questions by the Clerk or Chairman to the proposed surety.

Finally, in six cases, the Clerk explained to the intending surety the full implications which were involved in the procedure, so that he should realize the responsibilities that were being undertaken, and know what action could be taken in the event of no longer wishing to act as the defendant's surety.

The conclusions seem to be clear. When the magistrates decided to release a person on bail in his own recognisance, they appeared to have confidence in the soundness of this primary decision, and only in very exceptional cases did they take the secondary step of imposing an additional financial sanction in the form of a recognisance for a large sum of money; in most cases they merely requested a recognisance in a token sum of between £10–£25. Similarly, in cases where the magistrates required additional sureties from the defendant, they tended not to rely on the financial aspect of these sureties, rarely requiring more than a total of £100, from defendant and sureties together, but rather showed concern for ensuring the personal reliability and responsibility of the surety for the defendant's appearance at court.

This apparent lack of emphasis and lack of reliance upon the financial aspect of bail, which was observed in these English courts, seemed both fair and effective. During observation, there was no instance of anyone being unable to find the required sureties, and in the sample of 416 remand cases there were only two recorded examples of temporary remands in custody because sureties could not be contacted immediately. The Home Office Research Unit (1960) confirms that the number of persons remanded in custody solely because of an inability to find the requisite sureties is very small[1].

All the evidence, therefore, suggests that this aspect of the system works well, and it naturally raises the question of whether or not bail, with or without sureties, could be extended without risk to more persons awaiting trial. This question will be returned to in the final chapter.

---

1. Home Office Research Unit, *Time Spent Awaiting Trial,* p. 34 and Table 36: 26 persons were stated to have been remanded in custody because they were unable to find sureties—this was one per cent of persons committed for trial in custody, and 7 per cent of persons remanded in custody during summary trial. It was also added that '. . . in seven of these cases, the police opposed bail, so that lack of sureties may not have been the only reason for custody, although it was the reason stated.'

5. POLICE OPPOSITION TO BAIL

The first national statistics, for England and Wales, which drew attention to the fact that magistrates rarely granted bail to persons, when the police opposed bail, were those published in *Time Spent Awaiting Trial* (Home Office Research Unit, 1960). In that survey of a representative sample of courts throughout the country, it was found that magistrates granted bail to 95 per cent of the defendants, where there was no police opposition to bail, but, on the other hand, to only 8 per cent where the police objected to bail; in all cases where the police attitude was known, the magistrates acted contrary to the police recommendations in only 6 per cent of them.

It has already been noted, in Chapter 4, that a very similar situation was observed in the courts studied in this research, and that in the great majority of their decisions to grant or refuse bail the magistrates seemed to act in accordance with the implicit or explicit recommendations of the police.

Confirmation that the observed cases were not by any means atypical of the courts chosen for study was found, by analyzing the larger sample of cases drawn from the urban court in 1964.

The police opposed bail in 408 cases (64 per cent), and the magistrates granted bail to only 4 per cent of these persons, usually requiring additional sureties. A third of these cases were in Group A (Violence against the person) and, in fact, in this particular offence group over a fifth of the cases involving police opposition were granted bail.

It was known that there was no police opposition to bail in 182 cases (29 per cent): the magistrates did not refuse bail to any of these defendants, although in two instances persons were unable to find sureties and were therefore remanded in custody, temporarily, 'by default' as it were[1]. It was quite a common practice for the police, when not directly opposing bail, to request the magistrates

1. Thus less than 2 per cent of persons remanded in custody by the urban court were detained because they were unable to find sureties; this compares to the figure of 3.5 per cent in the Home Office Research Unit survey (1960).

to ask for sureties: this was done in almost 30 per cent of the cases in which there was no police opposition to bail *per se*.

The pattern of association between magistrates' decisions and police recommendation seems to be clear and consistent. This chapter will look more closely at the nature of police opposition to bail in the courts studied, and attempt to identify the main factors which were of concern to the police. Finally, this evidence will be considered in the light of certain legal aspects of bail decisions.

Police objections to bail: (a) Urban Court

During the period of observation at the urban court, June—August, 1965, although there were 76 cases in which the police requested a remand in custody, there were just fifty cases in which the police put forward specific objections to bail. Detailed notes were taken in court, recording the content of all these police objections, and subsequently the various reasons were classified to discover their frequency and distribution.

In each of the fifty cases, an average of three reasons for opposition to bail were put forward by the police; in twenty cases there was one reason which was emphasized as the most important[1], but in the remaining 30 cases all the reasons seemed to be of equal importance. Table 15 shows the frequency with which different factors were mentioned by the police, when objecting to bail. This simple breakdown of the content of police objections is of some interest as it stands, with perhaps a surprisingly high incidence of reasons connected with further police inquiries, but, because several reasons were put forward in each case by the police, it is important to examine more closely whether all the reasons in a case tended to be associated with each other or whether each case usually included several different ones.

TABLE 15

Reasons for police objections to bail in observed cases: Urban Court, 1965

Reasons for objections to bail	% of cases
Further charges	58
Criminal record	48
Other suspects to trace	34
Seriousness of the offence	26
Admits offence	24
No fixed abode	24
Found in possession of property	20
Unemployed	18
Threats to witnesses	16
Arrested 'on-the-job'	12
Likelihood of absconding	10
Other reasons	16
[Total number of cases =]	[50]

1. The most important reasons in these cases were as follows: seriousness of the offence—7 cases; threat to witnesses—4; arrested 'on-the-job' or in possession of stolen property—4; criminal record—3; further charges—1; no fixed abode—1.

Content analysis of the police objections identified fourteen separate reasons that were used. These reasons could be grouped into six more or less homogeneous categories, and the chart (below) shows these main categories with the specific reasons which each incorporates.

Main category	Specific reasons
1. *Non-appearance at trial.*	a. no fixed abode. b. unemployed. c. likelihood of absconding. d. no family ties. e. 'on-the-run' from the police.
2. *Seriousness of the offence.*	a. seriousness of the offence.
3. *Criminal record and further offences.*	a. previous convictions. b. will repeat the offence.
4. *Likelihood of guilt.*	a. admits the offence. b. found in possession of stolen property. c. arrested 'on-the-job'.
5. *Impeding police inquiries.*	a. further charges. b. found in possession of stolen property. c. other suspects to trace.
6. *Threats to witnesses.*	a. threats to witnesses.

Using this classification as a basis, it seemed important to attempt to answer the following questions: how often did all the reasons put forward by the police, in any one case, come from the same category? Where reasons from different categories were used, which categories were associated together? In what proportion of the total number of cases was at least one reason from a particular category used? Each of the six main categories will be considered with these questions in mind.

1. *Non-appearance at trial.*

Although there were five different factors, mentioned by the police, which might have suggested that the defendant would not appear to take his trial, yet two-thirds of all cases did not include any reason from this category. This meant that in the remaining one-third of the cases, the police often used two or three reasons together, all indicating a likelihood of non-appearance. Nevertheless, in all the cases in this category, reasons from other categories were used in addition, and there was only one case in which a non-appearance factor (viz. no fixed abode) was the *main* reason for police opposition to bail[1].

From Table 15 (above) it can be seen that the most common single reason in this category was 'no fixed abode' (n.f.a.), which was

1. Selected cases are recorded in full in Bottomley (1969), pp. 152–166, divided into examples of (a) *Police Opposition to Bail,* and (b) *Defence Solicitors' Applications for Bail.*

mentioned in 24 per cent of all cases; in a third of these n.f.a. cases, the other reasons were unconnected with non-appearance. Unemployment was a factor in 18 per cent of all cases, but in more than three-quarters of these cases it was supported by at least one other factor suggesting the likelihood of non-appearance. Similarly, in only one of the five cases where the police directly mentioned the risk of the defendant absconding were no other reasons for non-appearance put forward as objections to bail.

2. *Seriousness of the offence.*

The seriousness of the offence was mentioned in 26 per cent of all cases. In as many as half the cases where it was used, it was the *main* reason for police opposition to bail. In a quarter of the cases, the only other reason mentioned was the likelihood of a repetition of the offence, if the defendant was released on bail.

In only one of the cases was there any mention of a factor connected with non-appearance at trial, which suggests that the seriousness of the offence and non-appearance at trial were independent categories not often explicitly linked by the police in their opposition to bail. If any one factor had to be singled out for its association with the seriousness of the offence, it would be the likelihood of a repetition of the offence; in other words, in these cases the police may have seen the function and justification of arrest and pre-trial custody more generally in terms of the protection of the public rather than more narrowly in terms of the prevention of absconding before trial.

3. *Criminal record and further offences.*

In almost half the cases (48 per cent) of police opposition to bail, the defendant's previous criminal record was put forward as an objection. In a further 6 per cent of cases, the police said that he was likely to commit further offences.

More than 90 per cent of the criminal record cases included other objections concerned with the impeding of police enquiries or threats to witnesses; this suggests that the main rationale behind police objections to bail based on the defendant's criminal record was that such a person was more likely to impede police inquiries and tamper with the prosecution witnesses. The second main category associated with this one was that of non-appearance at trial: 37 per cent of the cases in this category included objections to bail based on the likelihood of non-appearance at trial; or, expressed another way round, six out of ten of the cases including a factor concerned with non-appearance also included an objection based on the defendant's criminal record.

It does not seem that the main concern of the police in these cases was the fear of further offences being committed, as in the few cases where this reason was put forward there was no mention of the defendant's previous criminal record; nor does it seem that the police put forward the criminal record mainly as a supporting factor pointing to the defendant's guilt, as in only one-fifth of these cases was any reason from the main category of 'likelihood of guilt' mentioned in association with the previous criminal record.

4. *Likelihood of guilt.*

Three factors, which implied that the defendant was likely to be guilty of the offence charged, were included in this category; they were (a) an alleged admission of the offence, (b) the fact that stolen property had been found in the defendant's possession, and (c) that the defendant had been arrested 'on-the-job', usually cases of 'breaking and entering', where the man was found on the premises by the police.

At least one of these three reasons was used in as many as 38 per cent of all cases: in over a third of these cases, two or more of the reasons suggesting likelihood of guilt were used together. It was not, however, a category of reason often used on its own, as in more than three-quarters of these cases reasons from other categories were put forward as additional police objections to bail. In more than two-thirds of the cases the other reasons included the hampering of police inquiries.

As was mentioned in the previous section, there seemed to be only a tenuous association between police objections based on the likelihood of guilt and those based on the fact that the defendant had a criminal record, as in only a quarter of the cases in this main category was the criminal record also put forward as an objection to bail. Similarly, there was very little evidence that the police believed that the likelihood of conviction would encourage a man to abscond before trial, as there were only three cases in which any factor concerned with non-appearance at trial was used with any factor suggesting the defendant's guilt.

5. *Impeding police inquiries.*

The three factors included in this category were (a) further charges were likely to be preferred, (b) stolen property had to be recovered or identified, and (c) there were other suspects still to be traced, in connection with the same offence.

At least one of these reasons was used in more than three-quarters of the cases (76 per cent). In 42 per cent of cases in this category, two or three reasons were used together, but in more than nine out of ten of the cases additional reasons from other categories were also included as police objections. The defendant's criminal record was mentioned as an additional reason in more than half these cases, probably being used by the police to give extra weight and credibility to their claim that the defendant would impede their inquiries.

Because of the very frequent occurrence of this type of reason in police objections to bail, it is perhaps of interest to note that all the seven cases which did *not* include reasons connected with police inquiries or threats to witnesses had a single main reason for police opposition to bail: in five of the cases it was the seriousness of the offence, and in the other two cases it was the likelihood of guilt.

6. *Threats to witnesses.*

In only 16 per cent of the cases did the police object to bail because there was a danger of witnesses being threatened. This was the least frequently used category, but its importance is shown by the fact that in half the cases where it was used it was the main reason for police opposition to bail. In three-quarters of the cases, the defendant's criminal record was mentioned to support the police fear for the safety of witnesses.

Before considering the evidence from the rural courts, it will be useful at this point to summarize, in tabular form, the material which has been reviewed from the observation in the urban court. Table 16 shows the frequency with which reasons from the six main categories were used (column a) and in what combinations, and also the proportion of cases in which they were the main police objection to bail (column b).

TABLE 16

Police objections to bail in the observed cases at the Urban Court, 1965: percentage of cases in which reasons from the main categories were used in combination

(See below, left, for six categories)

Reasons for police objections to bail	1.	2.	3.	4.	5.	6.	% of *all cases* (a) [n=50]	Main reason (b)
1. Non-appearance at trial	—	2	20	6	28	8	34	2
2. Seriousness of offence	2	—	14	10	14	4	26	14
3. Criminal record	20	14	—	10	40	12	54	6
4. Likelihood of guilt	6	10	10	—	26	2	38	8
5. Police inquiries	28	14	40	26	—	6	76	6
6. Threats to witnesses	8	4	12	2	6	—	16	8

Police objections to bail: (b) *Rural Courts.*

In the periods of observation at the three rural courts, between April–December, 1966, there were seventeen cases in which the police put forward specific objections to bail, with an average of rather less than three reasons in each case. In five cases there was one main reason: these were 'no fixed abode' (2 cases), offences committed on bail (2), and the defendant's criminal record (1).

Table 17 shows the frequency with which the different factors were mentioned by the police when objecting to bail; for comparable figures from the urban court, see Table 15 (above). The main differences between the urban and the rural courts appear to be the greater frequency of police objections based upon 'no fixed abode' and 'likelihood of absconding', in the rural courts, and the appearance of two new factors which did not feature in the urban court cases, viz. that the offence had been committed while already on bail, and that there were no sureties acceptable to the police. In the brief discussion which follows, of the main categories of police objections, 'no suitable sureties' will be included in category one, as indicating a risk of non-appearance at trial, and the fact that the offence had been committed on bail will be included in category three, as suggesting that the defendant might commit still further offences if released on bail again. When comparisons are made between the urban and rural courts in this section, it must be kept in mind that the number of cases observed at the rural courts was considerably smaller than at the urban.

TABLE 17

Reasons for police objections to bail in observed cases: Rural Courts, 1966

Reasons for objections to bail	% of cases
No fixed abode	47
Further charges	41
Criminal record	41
Likelihood of absconding	41
Seriousness of the offence	18
Offences on bail	18
No suitable sureties	18
Admits offence	12
Repetition of offence	12
Unemployed	6
Other reasons	6
[Total number of cases =]	[17]

1. *Non-appearance at trial.* At least one of the reasons concerned with the likelihood of the defendant's appearance at trial was mentioned in almost two-thirds of the cases (65 per cent). This was almost twice the frequency found in the urban court. In half these cases, at least two of the reasons in this category were used together; in two of the eleven cases, both the reasons for police opposition to bail were concerned with non-appearance, and in two further cases 'no fixed abode' was the *main* reason.

2. *Seriousness of the offence.* This objection to bail was mentioned in three of the cases (18 per cent), although in no instance was it the main reason. In only one case was a 'non-appearance' reason used

in association with the seriousness of the offence, and the additional reasons included previous criminal record (2 cases), and impending police inquiries (2 cases).

3. *Criminal record and further offences.* The defendant's previous criminal record or the likelihood that he would commit further offences, if released, were mentioned as objections to bail in 59 per cent of the cases—slightly more than at the urban court. In one case, the previous criminal record was the main objection to bail, and in two cases the fact of having committed the offence on bail was the main objection to further bail.

In the urban court, the main category associated with objections based on the accused's criminal record was that of impeding police inquiries; this was not found in the rural courts, where only one case included objections of a criminal record together with that of impeding police inquiries; but five of the seven cases of previous criminal records also included reasons suggesting that the offender would not appear to take his trial.

4. *Likelihood of guilt.* There were only two cases in the rural courts (12 per cent) where the police used a person's admission of guilt as a reason for objecting to bail; in both cases additional reasons suggested the likelihood of non-appearance. There were no cases in which the other reasons implying probable conviction (e.g. being in possession of stolen property, or arrested 'on-the-job') were mentioned by the police in the rural courts.

5. *Impeding police inquiries.* The only reason in this category, specified in police objections, was that of there being further charges: this was mentioned in 41 per cent of all cases. Contrary to the findings in the urban court, the defendant's criminal record was only mentioned in one of these seven cases; in four of the cases, a factor suggesting non-appearance was mentioned, and in another the likelihood of further offences.

6. *Threats to witnesses.* There was no example from the rural courts of police objecting to bail because of possible threats to witnesses.

To summarize the relatively small amount of material obtained from the rural courts, Table 18 simply shows the frequency with

TABLE 18

Police objections to bail in the observed cases at the Rural Courts, 1966: percentage of cases in which reasons from the main categories were used.

Reasons for police objections to bail	(a) % of all cases [n = 17]	(b) Main reason
1. Non-appearance at trial	65	12
2. Seriousness of the offence	18	—
3. Criminal record and further offences	59	18
4. Likelihood of guilt	12	—
5. Impeding police inquiries	41	—
6. Threats to witnesses	—	—

which reasons from the six main categories were used in the seventeen observed cases (column a) and the proportion of cases in which they were the main police objections to bail (column b).

Before examining the extent to which police objections to bail were related to legal aspects of the bail decision, it seems appropriate to consider the content of the applications *for* bail made by the defendant's solicitor, in the face of police opposition.

Applications for bail by the defendants

In Chapter 4 it was seen that most information was provided in those cases where a defendant was legally represented and his solicitor applied for bail, against police opposition (above p. 52). In this section, these twenty-six cases will be examined to see what factors were put forward by the Defence Solicitors, to justify the granting of bail to their clients, and to see how these factors compare with those put forward by the police who opposed bail.

In each of these applications for bail, an average of more than four reasons were given by the solicitors. Table 19 shows what the different reasons were and the frequency with which they were mentioned by the Defence Solicitors.

TABLE 19

Reasons for applications for bail by defendants' solicitors in observed cases at the Urban and Rural Courts, 1965–66

Reasons for bail	% of cases
Permanent residence	65
Sureties available	58
Regular employment/business commitments	50
No likelihood of absconding	46
Wife and family to support	46
Denies offence	42
No likelihood of further offences	31
Irrelevant criminal record	27
Assisted police inquiries	15
Will not impede inquiries	15
To prepare defence	12
Other reasons	15
[Total number of cases =]	[26]

These reasons can be grouped into a smaller number of categories, in a similar way to the reasons for police objections, with four main categories, corresponding, to a certain extent, to the police objections in categories 1, 3, 4 and 5. The chart (below) shows the main categories, and the specific reasons included in each.

Main category	Specific reasons
1. *Appearance at trial.*	a. permanent residence.
	b. sureties available.
	c. regular employment/business commitments.
	d. no likelihood of absconding.
	e. wife/family to support.
2. *Criminal record and further offences.*	a. irrelevant criminal record.
	b. no likelihood of further offences.
3. *Denial of the offence.*	a. denies the offence.
4. *Cooperation with the police.*	a. assisted police inquiries.
	b. will not impede further inquiries.

1. *Appearance at trial.* In more than 90 per cent of the applications, at least one of the factors suggesting the likelihood of appearance at trial was mentioned by the defendant's solicitor; in 81 per cent of all cases, at least two of these reasons were used, and in as many as 62 per cent three or more reasons. However, it is significant that in only a third of these cases had the police objected to bail on any ground connected with likely non-appearance, and in every one of these there were also police objections of other kinds.

2. *Criminal record and further offences.* In over half the cases, the Defence Solicitor claimed that his client's criminal record was not relevant to the present charge, that his last offence was a long time ago, or that it was most unlikely that he would commit any further offences, if released on bail. In four-fifths of these cases the police had, in fact, objected to bail because of the defendant's criminal record or the likelihood of further offences being committed. In the only three urban cases where the police objected to bail because of a likely recurrence of the offence, the defendant's solicitor, perhaps not surprisingly, specifically repudiated this allegation.

3. *Denial of the offence.* In eleven cases (42 per cent), the solicitor said that his client denied the offence and would be contesting the case. This type of reason, in support of an application for bail, was the opposite side of the coin to the police objection based on the accused's likelihood of guilt, and in none of the cases in which the defendant denied the offence, through his solicitor, did the police oppose bail on any of the grounds implying his guilt. However, it was of interest to find that, in all but two of the eleven cases, one of the grounds for police opposition was the accused's criminal record.

4. *Cooperation with the police.* In seven of the applications, it was stated that the defendant had cooperated with the police, or that he would not impede their further inquiries. This was usually to counter a police request for a remand in custody to safeguard their further inquiries, as in five of the seven cases some of the police objections to bail were concerned with the impeding of police inquiries.

This brief survey of the content of the Defence Solicitors' applications for bail suggests some tentative conclusions.

The most definite finding was that solicitors usually relied upon factors related to the domestic and community stability of their client, to support their claim that he was most unlikely to abscond, but this was in the face of opposition from the police who rarely disputed such facts, and only suggested the likelihood of absconding in a third of these cases. It was a common occurrence to hear cases in which the police objected to bail only or mainly because of the seriousness of the offence, or because of possible interference with witnesses and other police inquiries, and in which the solicitor then proceeded to apply for bail on the grounds of his client's domestic ties, without any attempt to answer or refute the specific police objections. For example, during observation at the urban court, in as many as half the cases where the Defence Solicitor applied for bail, one of the police objections was the seriousness of the offence, and in over a third of the cases part of the police opposition was based on the danger of threats to witnesses. In fact, there were only five of the twenty urban cases in which neither the seriousness of the offence nor threats to witnesses featured in the police objections, but in none of the remaining cases did the solicitor directly answer the police objections, so that in such cases an application for bail which stressed only that the defendant would appear for trial was not very likely to be successful. Similarly, in fifteen of the urban and rural cases, the police objected to bail because of further inquiries, and in only five of these was there any kind of refutation from the solicitor, showing that his client had cooperated with the police and would not impede their further inquiries.

The main type of case in which the solicitor directly replied to the police was that in which the police objected to bail on the grounds of the accused's criminal record or the likelihood of him committing further offences. These objections were used in almost three-quarters (73 per cent) of the cases in which a solicitor applied for bail, and in two-thirds of them the solicitor argued that the criminal record was irrelevant or that there was no likelihood of further offences being committed.

Finally, a small number of cases included a miscellaneous group of reasons which did not correspond to any of the main categories of police objections. For example, in one case observed at the urban court, the main reason put forward by a solicitor requesting bail for his client was so that witnesses for the defence could be traced, whom the defendant knew by sight but not by name; and there were, in all, three cases in which a remand in custody was shown to be particularly inconvenient for the preparation of the accused's defence.

Conclusions: legal aspects and police practice

From the analysis of the content of police objections to bail in the urban and rural courts, it has been possible to reach some tentative conclusions about the main factors which seemed to influence police recommendations. This final section will consider the extent to which observed police practice was related to certain legal aspects of the bail decision, as reflected in legislation and reported cases. Although it should not automatically be assumed that, because the magistrates acted in accordance with police recommendations in over 90 per cent of the cases, therefore they entirely agreed with the reasons put forward by the police, yet these stated police reasons can be seen as also indicating the factors most probably taken into account by the magistrates.

An examination of the statutes which have regulated the granting of bail in English law, before the Criminal Justice Act, 1967, showed that since 1835 the only statutory justification for the refusal of bail had been the likelihood that a defendant would not appear to take his trial (Bottomley, 1968). Several reported cases, particularly during the nineteenth century, confirmed this principle but also argued that other factors, such as the seriousness of the offence and the likelihood of guilt, could properly be taken into account when considering the likelihood of appearance at trial.[1]

However, in the analysis of police objections to bail at the urban court, it was found that only a third of the cases had any mention of factors suggesting the likelihood of non-appearance at trial; when, in comparison, more than half the cases had references to the defendant's previous criminal record and three-quarters to the impeding of police inquiries, it did not seem that the police at the urban court were mainly concerned with the risk of non-appearance.

From the smaller amount of evidence available from the rural courts, it seemed that this factor was more important in the rural area, perhaps because the criminal population was more unsettled and the risk of absconding correspondingly higher: in the three rural courts studied, two-thirds of the cases included a mention of factors in this category. This part of East Anglia was one in which much petty crime was committed by 'travelling' gypsies, van-dwellers and persons engaged in seasonal agricultural work.

When the police opposed bail for reasons other than the risk of absconding before trial, they did not exactly link these other factors to the risk of absconding. Thus, in only one case at the urban court was the seriousness of the offence mentioned together with the likelihood of non-appearance, and in only three urban cases was the likelihood of guilt used in conjunction with it. At the rural courts,

1. See, for example, *R. v. Scaife*, (1841) 10 L.J.M.C. 144, and *R. v. Robinson*, (1854) 23 L.J.(Q.B.) 286. See also Archbold, *Pleading, Evidence and Practice in Criminal Cases*, (36th ed. London, 1966) §203.

the main factor mentioned in association with the likelihood of absconding was the defendant's criminal record.

The police seemed to accept that the seriousness of an offence justified the refusal of bail, irrespective of its possible connection with the risk of non-appearance. It was mentioned in a minority of cases, but in more than 10 per cent of all the cases it was the *main* reason for police opposition to bail. There was no other category frequently associated with this reason, although in three of the urban cases where the seriousness of the offence was the main reason, the supporting reason was the likelihood of a recurrence of the offence. It was used most frequently in offences of violence against the person, and it seemed likely that in this type of case the rationale behind the police attitude was that it was important to protect the public from further possible crimes of violence by remanding accused persons in custody.

The Court of Criminal Appeal has laid down that magistrates should refuse bail to persons with long criminal records, who are likely to commit further offences on bail[1]; and, as a necessary corollary to this, it has also been stated that a court is justified in hearing evidence of a defendant's criminal record before deciding about bail[2]. In more than half the cases where they opposed bail, the police put forward the defendant's criminal record as an objection, or claimed that he was likely to commit further offences if released on bail. At the urban court, in more than 90 per cent of the cases in which the criminal record was mentioned, there were additional objections connected with the hampering of police inquiries or possible threats to witnesses; this suggests that the police submitted evidence of the accused's record to support their claim that he was likely to impede their inquiries, and not necessarily to suggest that he might commit further offences on bail.

For a long time, from the early Statute of Westminster (1275) to a statute of 1826 (7 Geo. 4 c. 64), it was repeated that, where the guilt of the accused was certain or very probable, bail could properly be refused. This consideration was repudiated in 1835 (by 5 and 6 Will. c. 33 s. 3), and since then has not appeared in any of the statutes concerning bail. Similarly, when factors suggesting the guilt of the accused have occurred in reported cases, it has been stated that they are only to be considered as supporting evidence for the likelihood of absconding. Nevertheless, in the urban court, the police mentioned factors suggesting probable guilt in 38 per cent of the cases, which was more frequent than the mention of factors suggesting the likelihood of non-appearance. In only 6 per cent of the urban cases were these two factors mentioned together, which indic-

1. *R. v. Phillips*, (1947) 32 Cr. App. R. 47; see also *R. v. Wharton*, [1955] *Crim. L.R.* 565.
2. *R. v. Dyson*, (1943) 195 L.T.R. (O.S.) 237; *R. v. Fletcher*, (1947) 113 *J.P.* 365; *R. v. Armstrong*, (1951 2 All E.R. 219.

ated that the police did not necessarily see them as interrelated; and in as many as 8 per cent of the urban cases, the likelihood of guilt was the main reason for police opposition to bail. In more than two-thirds of the cases where this reason was used, other objections were based on the possible interference with police inquiries. More surprisingly, perhaps, it was found that in only 10 per cent of the urban cases was evidence of a defendant's criminal record submitted with other evidence suggesting guilt, and it seemed that these two factors were usually used in a mutually exclusive way, rather than being complementary.

The main conclusion from observation at the urban court is that in the great majority of cases where the police objected to bail, their major concern was with possible interference with their further inquiries. In more than three-quarters of the urban cases, factors concerned with police inquiries were mentioned as objections to bail. This particular type of reason has never been accepted as a justifiable ground for refusing bail in any statute nor even been acknowledged as a proper contributory factor in any officially reported case.

It was not often used by the police as the sole reason for opposing bail, but it was most frequently supported by evidence of the defendant's previous criminal record. The only type of case in which, occasionally, no mention was made of police inquiries was that in which there was another single *main* reason put forward by the police, such as the seriousness of the offence or possible threats to witnesses. In half the small group of urban cases in which the police mentioned the danger of interference with witnesses, this was their main reason for objecting to bail, and in three-quarters of these cases the police submitted additional evidence of the accused's previous criminal record.

In the light of this evidence, which may be typical of other urban courts in England, it would seem to be important for magistrates to receive guidance as to how to view cases of this kind. The situation was very well summed up, and the practical problems frankly stated, by a Metropolitan Magistrate, Mr. Richard Beddington, at the 'Justice' Conference on Bail and Remands in Custody, in November, 1965:

> The only reasons which are normally put forward [in opposing bail] . . . are the likelihood of a man answering to his bail or not, and the other one which is quite common, and which is much more difficult to deal with, is when the police say that there are further inquiries to make, there is the possibility of other charges to be preferred, there are other persons concerned and that the release of the man on bail may hamper their inquiries. In my short experience, that is the case which I find really difficult to

deal with. In practice, I do not think one can interfere too much with the practical side of it; we have to rely, I think, very much on what we are told by the officer in charge of the case when he opposes bail. If he says there are further enquiries to make we, in practice have to take that very seriously into consideration. I do not say that it is a 100 per cent obstacle to granting bail, but we have to take it seriously into consideration.

(U. S. A. 1965a, p. 201)

Similarly, Lord Devlin has pointed out that although possible interference with witnesses is an important factor to be considered in the decision about bail, yet it is one of the most difficult questions to deal with and may mean only that the police want the defendant out of the way while they complete their inquiries (Devlin, 1960).

The Criminal Justice Act, 1967, was a great disappointment in respect of guidance on these factors; not only is the range of cases covered by the restrictions on the refusal of bail (s. 18) rather limited, but the factors recognized as proper for consideration in these bail decisions do not include any factors concerned with the hampering of police inquiries or even with potential threats to witnesses. An original clause of the Bill stated that bail could be refused 'where by reason of other circumstances it appears to the court necessary in the interests of justice or for the protection of himself or others'; this clause, although unnecessarily vague, would have covered instances where police object to bail on the grounds of their further inquiries or interference with witnesses, but in the Committee Stage of the Bill it was replaced by two new clauses which, while more specific, only justify a refusal of bail—'12(g) where it appears to the court that unless he is remanded or committed in custody he is likely to commit an offence; or (h) where it appears to the court necessary for his own protection to refuse to remand or commit him on bail'. Thus, the position is no clearer than it was before, and magistrates are left without any guidance or help as to how they should deal with the cases in which the police oppose bail on grounds of possible interference with their further inquiries or with witnesses.

6. SOCIAL AND CRIMINAL CHARACTERISTICS OF REMAND PRISONERS

Several aspects of the decision-making process, whereby magistrates remanded persons in custody before trial, have already been described. The examination of the amount and type of information available to the magistrates at the time of making their decisions (Chapter 4), and the content analysis of police objections to bail (Chapter 5), both shed some light on the factors which may have determined whether or not a particular person was remanded in custody. Another approach to the same problem is to analyse the social and criminal characteristics of persons remanded in custody, in order to see what differences, if any, there were between them and those released on bail by the magistrates. It was possible to carry out such an investigation of the sample of remand cases at the urban and rural courts, during the period 1963–65; but, before the findings are presented, some preliminary comments must be made about the exact nature of the exercise and the type of conclusions that can be properly drawn.

The information which provided the basis of the analysis was drawn from all the documentary sources available for each case (see Appendix); these included not only the Court Papers for the magistrates' court hearing, but also the C. I. D. files and 'antecedent histories' prepared for higher court trial (where applicable). There is no guarantee that all, or indeed any, of this information was brought to the attention of the magistrates at the time when they were making their decision; in fact, from the evidence of personal observation of such decisions in the same courts, it seems most unlikely that the magistrates would have known all the relevant information in a majority of the cases. It is, however, probable that more of the information would have been known to the police at the time, and may have influenced police recommendations. Although this analysis cannot provide direct evidence about the mechanics of the decision-making process in the courts, it can indicate the extent to which the magistrates' decisions were successful in remanding in custody persons with different characteristics from those whom they decided to release on bail; thus it will be possible to see whether these decisions were largely arbitrary in their results or whether they successfully distinguished between people with different characteristics.

In order that the distinction between bail and custody cases should be as well defined as possible for the purpose of this analysis, the urban and rural cases were divided into three groups:

(i) those who were always remanded on bail;
(ii) those always remanded in custody;
(iii) those remanded partly on bail and partly in custody;

in this way, the main comparisons could concentrate on the differences between groups (i) and (ii). After the sample had been reweighted, to take account of the different sampling fractions of the offence groups at the urban court, this division resulted in the following figures:

(i) 270 persons (32 per cent) were always remanded on bail;
(ii) 476 persons (56 per cent) were always remanded in custody;
(iii) 108 persons (13 per cent) were remanded partly on bail and partly in custody.

When the urban and the rural cases were compared, it was found that more were remanded in custody by the urban court: 59 per cent of the urban cases were always remanded in custody, compared to less than 46 per cent of the rural, whereas only 29 per cent of the urban cases were always on bail, compared to over 40 per cent of the rural. This difference was in no way affected by the previously noted fact that more of the rural cases were eventually committed for trial to a higher court, because analysis showed that both in cases tried summarily and in cases committed for trial, the urban court remanded in custody 12–15 per cent more than the rural courts. It seemed, therefore, that the analysis of the background characteristics of persons remanded in custody should not only investigate differences between those in custody and those on bail, but at the same time it should investigate whether there were any differences between the urban and rural cases which might 'explain' the greater proportion remanded in custody by the urban court magistrates.

The following characteristics were examined: 1. nature of the offence; 2. previous criminal record; 3. employment; 4. family ties.

1. *Nature of the offence*

The sample was selected on the basis of three main offence groups:

Group A: Violence against the person;
Group B: Larceny and False Pretences;
Group C: Breaking and Entering Offences.

Table 20 shows the percentages on bail and in custody, according to these three offence groups. There is a progressive trend, from Group A through to Group C: one-third of Group A were always remanded in custody, compared to three-quarters of Group C. This seems to indicate that the general nature of the offence had a strong bearing on the chances of being remanded in custody, and provides initial confirmation of the Home Office Research Unit's finding that a greater proportion of persons charged with 'breaking and entering' offences were remanded in custody (Home Office Research Unit, 1960, Tables 3, 4 and 18). It cannot, of course, be ruled out at this stage that there may have been a more important intervening variable associated with being remanded in custody, which occurred with different frequency in the offence groups, thereby explaining away this apparent relationship. The effect of one such possible variable, previous criminal record, will be considered in the next section.

A comparison between the urban and rural cases, according to the offence (Table 20), shows that in each group at least 6 per cent

TABLE 20

Persons remanded in custody and on bail, according to the main offence groups

Offence Group	TOTAL	BAIL		CUSTODY		BAIL & CUSTODY	
	no.	%	(no.)	%	(no.)	%	(no.)
URBAN COURT							
A (Violence)	57	49·1	(28)	33·4	(19)	17·5	(10)
B (Larcenies)	280	42·9	(120)	40·0	(112)	17·1	(48)
C (Breakings)	304	11·8	(36)	81·5	(248)	6·6	(20)
Total	641	28·7	(184)	59·1	(379)	12·2	(78)
RURAL COURTS							
A (Violence)	18	55·5	(10)	27·8	(5)	16·7	(3)
B (Larcenies)	116	48·3	(56)	45·7	(53)	6·0	(7)
C (Breakings)	79	25·3	(20)	49·4	(39)	25·3	(20)
Total	213	40·4	(86)	45·5	(97)	14·1	(30)
ALL CASES							
A (Violence)	75	50·7	(38)	32·0	(24)	17·3	(13)
B (Larcenies)	396	44·4	(176)	41·7	(165)	13·9	(55)
C (Breakings)	383	14·6	(56)	75·0	(287)	10·4	(40)
Grand Total	854	31·6	(270)	55·7	(476)	12·7	(108)

Tests of significance[1] Offence Groups A and B compared with Group C:
(i) Urban Court: $chi^2 = 102{\cdot}4$ ($P \angle 0{\cdot}001$)
(ii) Rural Courts: $chi^2 = 5{\cdot}2$ ($P \angle 0{\cdot}025$)
(iii) All Cases: $chi^2 = 106{\cdot}9$ ($P \angle 0{\cdot}001$)

1. In this and the subsequent tests for statistical significance, the tables have been reduced to a 2 × 2 form and Yates' Correction of the chi^2 test used. The mixed, bail and custody, cases have not therefore been included in these tests.

fewer were released on bail by the urban court, although in Group B (Larcenies) more were remanded in custody *all the time* by the rural courts than by the urban court, because there were more at the urban court who spent just *part* of their remand period in custody. The greatest difference was found in Group C (Breaking and Entering), where more than four-fifths of those at the urban court spent all the time in custody compared to only half at the rural courts. In fact, if the comparison between the urban and rural courts is restricted to Groups A and B, then the differences between them are reduced by more than half.

It is impossible to be in any way dogmatic about the importance of the actual offence, simply on the basis of the proportions remanded in custody in these three broad offence groups, without some attempt to investigate possible aspects of the offences themselves which may be significant. A certain amount of information was available, which enabled a closer analysis of the offence groups to be carried out. This analysis was in two parts: in the first place, certain aspects of the nature of the offences were examined, such as the legal classifications, the surrounding circumstances, and the value of any stolen property; in the second place, the offences were considered according to the police inquiries surrounding them, investigating such factors as whether other suspects had still to be traced, and whether any offences were taken into consideration at the time of sentencing. Further details of the nature of the offences in each group will be considered first.

Group A included four separate offences, in the following legal classifications:

(i) wounding with intent to cause grievous bodily harm (Offences Against the Person Act, 1861, s. 18);
(ii) inflicting grievous bodily harm (O. A. P. A. s. 20);
(iii) occasioning actual bodily harm (O. A. P. A. s. 47);
(iv) possessing an offensive weapon.

Over half the group faced an initial charge of s. 18 wounding, and together with the s. 20 woundings these two offences formed almost three-quarters of the whole group. Slightly fewer than average were released on bail in these two offences, with a greater than average proportion released on bail of those charged with s. 47 assault and possessing an offensive weapon; but very similar proportions were detained in custody *all the time* on remand, in each of the four offences.

A 'situational classification' of offences of violence against the person, which has been developed by the Institute of Criminology, Cambridge, was used in an attempt to see whether any particular aspects of the circumstances of the offence influenced the likelihood of being remanded in custody or on bail[1]. Table 21 shows the numbers on bail and in custody, according to the circumstances of their offence.

TABLE 21

Situational classification of offences in Group A, according to whether the remand was on bail or in custody

Circumstances of offence	TOTAL	Bail	Custody	Bail & Custody
1. Sexual attack on stranger	3	1	2	—
2. Result of a family dispute, away from the home.	9	2	4	3
3. Domestic quarrel, in or around the home.	10	8	2	—
4. Dispute between fellow-workers	4	2	2	—
5. Attacks in or around pubs, cafes, etc:				
(a) on stranger or staff	21	12	6	3
(b) on person known.	3	2	1	—
6. Attacks in street or public place:				
(a) on stranger.	13	8	2	3
(b) on person known	8	3	2	3
7. Other types of attack	4	—	3	1
Total	75	38	24	13

No clearly defined trends appear from this analysis. Although as many as eight out of ten were released on bail when the offence resulted from a domestic quarrel in or around the home, yet only two out of nine were granted bail when it was the result of a family dispute away from the home. If attacks in the street or public places are considered, eight out of the thirteen involving strangers were released on bail, compared to only three out of eight involving persons already known to the accused; in this instance, a partial explanation may be found in the relative seriousness of the offences, as six of the eight attacks on known persons were initially s. 18 charges, compared to only two of the thirteen involving strangers. However, if the whole group is divided into those offences which involved persons known to the accused and those which involved strangers, identical proportions were remanded on bail and in custody.

All that can be said on the basis of this inconclusive evidence, is that persons who were involved in family quarrels away from the home and the (probably associated) category of persons attacking known persons in the street or other public places, were less likely than average to be released on bail.

Group B included all the larcenies, false pretences and related offences in Classes III and V of the Home Office Statistical Classification, with the additional offence of 'taking and driving away a

1. See F. H. McClintock, assisted by N. H. Avison et al, *Crimes of Violence*, (London, 1963), Ch. 2.

motor vehicle without the consent of the owner'. Fifty-six per cent of all the offences in the group were simple larcenies; the only other offence groups of any size were—taking and driving away (11 per cent), larceny in a dwelling house (9 per cent), receiving stolen property (7 per cent), and larceny by a servant (6 per cent).

In the group as a whole, 42 per cent were remanded in custody and 44 per cent were released on bail. More than average were remanded in custody, charged with the following offences: obtaining by a false pretence—65 per cent in custody; taking and driving away a motor vehicle—55 per cent. More than average were released on bail, charged with the following offences: larceny by a servant—87 per cent on bail; receiving stolen property—56 per cent.

Information was usually available about the value of the stolen property, and this seemed a likely criterion to be associated with bail or custody. Table 22 shows the relationship between the value of the stolen property and whether the remand was on bail or in custody.

TABLE 22

Persons in Group B remanded on bail or in custody, according to the value of the stolen property.

Value of stolen property	TOTAL (no.)	Bail (%)	Custody (%)	Bail & Custody (%)
∠ £10	147	66·7	27·2	6·1
£10 ∠ £50	81	28·4	49·4	22·2
£50 ∠ £100	41	51·2	29·3	19·5
£100 ∠ £500	45	13·3	64·5	22·5
£500 or more	35	42·9	40·0	17·1
not known/not applicable	(47)	(27·6)	(63·9)	(8·5)
TOTAL	396	44·4	41·7	13·9

Thirty-seven per cent of all cases in Group B involved less than £10, and only one-fifth involved £100 or more. Apart from the fact that two-thirds of those who stole less than £10 were released on bail, there was no consistent relationship between the value of the stolen property and the likelihood of being remanded in custody: more than average were remanded in custody of those who stole £10 ∠ £50, and also £100 ∠ £500, but less than average were detained in custody of those stealing £50 ∠ £100 and £500 or more.

Group C included several different types of breaking and entering; although the differences between the offences were not very great, more than average were remanded in custody of those charged with warehousebreaking and burglary, and less than average of those charged with housebreaking. Reclassifying the cases, according to a more exact description of the type of property entered, developed by Chappell (1965), it was still found that in cases involving dwelling houses and 'combined dwelling and sale premises' fewer persons were remanded in custody.

There was no relationship between the value of the property stolen in the breaking and entering offences, and the likelihood of being remanded in custody.

To summarize the main conclusions of this investigation into aspects of the nature of the offence which may have been related to the likelihood of being remanded in custody: the outstanding factor, which confirms earlier research, was simply that persons charged with any type of breaking and entering offence (Group C) were much more likely to be remanded in custody than persons charged with any other offence included in this survey; in Group A (Violence against the person), there was a slight tendency for persons charged with the more serious type of wounding to be remanded in custody, but there did not seem to be any discernible pattern whereby particular circumstances surrounding an offence might have influenced the remand decision; in Group B (Larceny and False Pretences), there was a considerable variation in the proportions remanded in custody in the separate offences included in this group, but persons charged with offences involving thefts of less than £10 were more likely to be granted bail, even though there was no *consistent* relationship between the value of stolen property and being remanded in custody.

The second part of this investigation into certain aspects of the offence, involved an examination of factors concerned with the police inquiries surrounding each offence. This seemed to be an important line of investigation, in view of the frequency with which the police had been observed to oppose bail because of the danger that their inquiries might be hampered (see Chapter 5). From the information that was available, it was possible to examine three aspects, in this connection: (i) other suspects still to be traced, (ii) alteration or additions to the initial charge, and (iii) offences taken into consideration.

(i) *Other suspects.* In 42 per cent of all cases, the offence was committed alone; in a further 47 per cent of the cases, all the suspects had been arrested together; so that in only 11 per cent of the cases were there other suspects still to be traced—and all but seven of these ninety-three cases were at the urban court. Eighty-five per cent of these cases at the urban court were detained in custody for all or part of their period on remand. This factor did not in any way contribute to the greater proportion remanded in custody in Group C, at the urban court, as not only was there a *smaller* proportion with other suspects to trace in this group (13 per cent) than in Group B (16 per cent), but over 80 per cent of those in Group B were remanded in custody all or part of the time.

(ii) *Charges.* In 69 per cent of the urban cases and 82 per cent of the rural cases, the initial charge remained unaltered throughout the remand hearings and proceedings up to and including the trial. The alterations in the remaining cases were either (a) where the initial charge was dropped and/or a less serious charge was preferred, or (b) where additional and/or more serious charges were preferred.

In the urban court, where the initial charge was dropped and replaced by less serious charges, almost one half were on bail and only a third remanded in custody; but where there were additional or more serious charges, almost three-quarters were remanded in custody all the time, and less than one-fifth were released on bail. Although there were slightly more with additional charges in Group C (24 per cent) than in Group B (17 per cent) or A (14 per cent), yet a much greater proportion of those in Group C were still remanded in custody (89 per cent) than in Group B (57 per cent) or A (13 per cent).

In the rural courts, the pattern was not as marked, but where more serious charges were preferred there were still slightly more persons remanded in custody.

(iii) *Offences taken into consideration (t.i.c).* A very consistent pattern was found in both the urban and the rural courts: where no offences were t.i.c. or suspected by the police, more than average were released on bail; there was then a gradual increase in the proportion remanded in custody, according to the number of offences t.i.c. Once again, the trend was more definite in the urban court, where it reached a high level of statistical significance (Table 23).

Group C included a smaller proportion of persons with no offences t.i.c. or suspected than the other two offence groups, and 30 per cent had offences t.i.c. (compared to 14 per cent in Group B, and none in

TABLE 23

Persons remanded on bail or in custody, according to the number of offences taken into consideration

	TOTAL		Bail		Custody		Bail & Custody	
	no.	(%)	no.	(%)	no.	(%)	no.	(%)
No offences t.i.c. or suspected	482	(56·5)	192	(39·8)	221	(45·9)	69	(14·3)
Other offences suspected	134	(15·7)	40	(29·8)	83	(62·0)	11	(8·2)
1∠5 offences t.i.c.	143	(16·8)	29	(20·3)	98	(68·5)	16	(11·2)
5 or more t.i.c.	93	(10·9)	7	(7·5)	74	(79·6)	12	(12·9)
(no information)	(2)		(2)					
Total	854	(100·0)	270	(31·6)	476	(55·7)	108	(12·7)

Tests of significance: Cases where no offences were t.i.c. or suspected, compared with those in which one or more further offences were t.i.c.:

(i) Urban Court: chi^2 = 52·3 (P ∠ 0·001)
(ii) Rural Courts: chi^2 = 2·7 (n.s.)
(iii) All cases: chi^2 = 49·4 (P ∠ 0·001)

Group A); but, nevertheless, twice the proportion of those with no offences t.i.c. were remanded in custody in Group C, compared to Groups A and B, and 86 per cent of those with offences t.i.c. were remanded in custody compared to only 60 per cent remanded in custody in Group B. Thus, although Group C had more cases with offences taken into consideration than the other offence groups, there were still proportionately more remanded in custody.

This limited evidence suggests that there was an association between various aspects of the police inquiries surrounding an offence and the incidence of remands in custody; this association was marked in cases where the accused subsequently had offences taken into consideration at sentence, and to a lesser extent where additional charges were preferred or where there were other suspects still to be traced. In each aspect, the urban cases showed more distinct patterns of association than did the rural courts, but when the offence groups were examined separately it was evident that none of these factors significantly contributed to explaining the greater proportion remanded in custody in Group C, Breaking and Entering.

2. *Previous criminal record*

Three-quarters of the cases at the urban court and two-thirds at the rural courts had previous criminal convictions for indictable offences; as many as 54 per cent of the urban and 43 per cent of the rural cases had three or more previous convictions. There was a very strong relationship between remands in custody and previous criminal record, as shown in Table 24. Sixty-three per cent of persons with no previous convictions were released on bail, all the time on remand, whereas only 13 per cent of those with three or more convictions were on bail all the time.

When the factor of the previous criminal record was taken into account, part of the difference between the urban and the rural courts disappeared: *all* the courts released on bail approximately 63 per cent of persons with no previous convictions, who constituted a quarter of the urban sample, but almost a third of the rural; however, when dealing with persons *with* criminal records, the urban court consistently remanded in custody 10–15 per cent more than did the rural courts. If an additional criterion, of having served a previous custodial sentence was used, the gap between the urban and rural courts narrowed slightly, as a greater proportion of those with criminal records at the urban court had served a custodial sentence.

In the previous section, it was seen that a greater proportion of persons charged with breaking and entering offences (Group C) were remanded in custody than other offence groups, and this difference was not explained by various factors that were examined concerned with additional charges, or offences subsequently taken into consideration. Because of the strong association which has been found between having a criminal record and the increased likelihood of being remanded in custody, it seemed important to examine the extent to which persons with criminal records were evenly distributed among the three offence groups, and whether this factor could explain the greater proportion remanded in custody in Group C.

As expected, it was found that 89 per cent of Group C had previous indictable convictions, compared to 64 per cent of Group B and 41 per cent of Group A; however, when this factor was controlled, comparable persons in Groups A and B were treated very much alike, but Group C still stood out as being the group in which significantly greater proportions of comparable persons were remanded in custody. A final analysis used the criterion of having served a custodial sentence: once again, this applied to 63 per cent of Group C, but only 36 per cent of Group B and 27 per cent of Group A; when this was controlled, although the difference between Group C and the other groups was even more significant for persons with *no*

TABLE 24

Persons remanded in custody and on bail, according to their previous criminal record

	TOTAL		No previous convictions		1 ∠ 3 previous convictions		3 or more previous convictions	
	no.	(%)	no.	(%)	no.	(%)	no.	(%)
URBAN COURT								
Bail	184	(28·7)	101	(63·5)	45	(32·6)	38	(11·0)
Custody	379	(59·1)	44	(27·7)	74	(53·6)	261	(75·9)
Bail & Custody	78	(12·2)	14	(8·8)	19	(13·8)	45	(13·1
Total	641	(100·0)	159	(24·8)	138	(21·5)	344	(53·7)
RURAL COURTS								
Bail	86	(40·4)	43	(62·3)	23	(44·2)	20	(21·7)
Custody	97	(45·5)	16	(23·2)	20	(38·5)	61	(66·3)
Bail & Custody	30	(14·1)	10	(14·5)	9	(17·3)	11	(12·0)
Total	213	(100·0)	69	(32·4)	52	(24·4)	92	(43·2)
ALL CASES								
Bail	270	(31·6)	144	(63·2)	68	(35·8)	58	(13·3)
Custody	476	(55·7)	60	(26·3)	94	(49·5)	322	(73·9)
Bail & Custody	108	(12·7)	24	(10·5)	28	(14·7)	56	(12·8)
Grand Total	854	(100·0)	228	(26·7)	190	(22·2)	436	(51·1)

Tests of significance: Cases with no previous convictions, compared with those with one or more previous convictions:

(i) Urban Court: chi^2 = 119·0 (P ∠ 0·001)
(ii) Rural Courts: chi^2 = 21·9 (P ∠ 0.001)
(iii) All Cases: chi^2 = 186·6 (P ∠ 0.001)

previous custodial sentence, yet the difference was very much reduced (to a level at which it was no longer statistically significant) when only those who had served a previous custodial sentence were considered.

The findings of this section would seem to emphasize the importance of a previous criminal record, and having served a previous custodial sentence; not only were these factors strongly associated with the likelihood of being remanded in custody, but they went some way towards 'explaining' why the urban courts remanded more in custody than the rural courts, and why more persons charged with breaking and entering (Group C) were remanded in custody than persons charged with offences of violence (Group A) or theft (Group B).

3. *Employment*

In its study, *Time Spent Awaiting Trial* (1960), the Home Office Research Unit emphasized the link between employment and bail; it found that two-thirds of those on bail were employed, but less than one-third of those in custody (Home Office Research Unit, 1960, Table 34). A more useful way of expressing this relationship would have been to say that three-quarters of persons in employment were released on bail, compared to 40 per cent of the unemployed. Table 25 shows the comparable figures for the urban and rural cases in our sample : only 42 per cent of persons in employment were always released on bail, but this compared to less than 18 per cent of those who were unemployed. Expressed the other way round, 74 per cent of persons on bail were employed, compared to 46 per cent of persons remanded in custody.

The proportion who were unemployed in the total sample was 43 per cent, which is very similar to the proportion of 46 per cent in the Home Office Research Unit's national sample. The urban and rural courts probably had about the same proportions unemployed, but the relationship between unemployment and remands in custody was stronger in the urban court : 73 per cent of the unemployed at the urban court were remanded in custody, compared to 56 per cent of those unemployed at the rural courts; and 48 per cent of those in employment were remanded in custody by the urban court, compared to 39 per cent at the rural courts.

Not only was there this strong relationship between unemployment and being remanded in custody, but for those who were employed there was a strong relationship between release on bail and the length of time they had been in their present employment. Of those who had been in their present job for less than four weeks, almost 70 per cent were always remanded in custody; but the proportion released on bail steadily increased with the length of the current employment, so that of those who had held their present job for twelve months or more only a quarter were remanded in custody. There was no corresponding relationship between the length of time a person had been *unemployed* and his chances of being granted bail.

4. *Family ties*

The Home Office Research Unit also analysed the number of persons on bail and in custody known to have dependants. Seventy per cent of persons known to have dependants were released on bail, compared to 51 per cent of persons known to have no dependants; or, expressed differently, 40 per cent of those on bail were known to have dependants compared to only 23 per cent of those remanded in custody. The limited conclusions drawn from this analysis were that:

> Persons on bail were more often known to have dependants than those in custody. This is not independent of the previous findings, since men with dependants are more likely to make an effort to obtain or keep employment... The figures suggest that magistrates may be more reluctant to remand or commit in custody when there are dependants, especially in the less serious cases; but it is also possible that those without dependants are of a different type.
>
> (Home Office Research Unit, 1960, p. 33)

TABLE 25

Persons remanded on bail and in custody, according to whether they were employed or unemployed

	TOTAL		Bail		Custody		Bail & Custody	
	no.	(%)	no.	(%)	no.	(%)	no.	(%)
URBAN COURT								
Employed	355	(55·4)	138	(38·8)	171	(48·2)	46	(13·0)
Unemployed	286	(44·6)	46	(16·1)	208	(72·7)	32	(11·2)
Total	641	(100·0)	184	(28·7)	379	(59·1)	78	(12·2)
RURAL COURTS								
Employed	120	(56·3)	62	(51·6)	47	(39·2)	11	(9·2)
Unemployed	82	(38·5)	19	(23·2)	46	(56·1)	17	(20·7)
not known	11	(5·2)	5	(45·4)	4	(36·4)	2	(18·2)
Total	213	(100·0)	86	(40·4)	97	(45·5)	30	(14·1)
ALL CASES								
Employed	475	(55·6)	200	(42·1)	218	(45·9)	57	(12·0)
Unemployed	368	(43·1)	65	(17·7)	254	(69·0)	49	(13·3)
not known	11	(1·3)	5	(45·4)	4	(36·4)	2	(18·2)
Grand Total	854	(100·0)	270	(31·6)	476	(55·7)	108	(12·7)

Tests of significance: (i) Urban Court: chi² = 43·5 (P ∠ 0.001)
(ii) Rural Courts: chi² = 11·5 (P ∠ 0·001)
(iii) All cases: chi² = 58·1 (P ∠ 0·001)

Considering the marital status of the sample, almost half, both in the urban and the rural courts, were single and not cohabiting at the time of their court appearance; more than average of this group were remanded in custody all the time (63 per cent). Thirty per cent of the sample were married, and living with their wives; less than 40 per cent of these were remanded in custody. A smaller group of 13 per cent were divorced or separated, and living alone; more than two-thirds of this group were remanded in custody.

The urban and rural courts had very similar proportions in each category, except that all the married immigrants (2.5 per cent of the total) occurred in the urban sample. In every category, except one, the urban court consistently remanded 10–12 per cent more in custody than did the rural courts.

A similar picture emerged from a classification of the cases according to their actual 'living situation' at the time of arrest. Over a fifth of the sample were living in lodgings; three-quarters of this group were remanded in custody all the time. A fifth were living with one or both parents, and more than average were released on bail (42 per cent). The police described 83 of the sample (10 per cent) as being of 'no fixed abode', and all but six of them were remanded in custody.

No more definite conclusions can be reached on the basis of this evidence than those of the Home Office Research Unit. In general terms, it has been confirmed that those with more permanent family relationships, who were living with relatives or dependants, were more often released on bail, whereas those who lived on their own, in lodgings or of 'no fixed abode', were much more likely to be remanded in custody. It cannot be certain whether, as seems likely, these factors had an independent influence on the magistrates' decisions (where the information was known to them), or whether they were related to other relevant factors such as unemployment or criminal record. The cases at the rural courts included rather more persons living with their parents and slightly fewer living in lodgings than the urban cases, but nevertheless the urban court always remanded more of each category in custody.

Conclusions

The two main aims of the analysis that has been described in this chapter were to compare the background characteristics of those remanded in custody with those released on bail, and, secondly, to see whether there were any material differences between the urban and the rural cases which might help to account for the greater proportion remanded in custody by the urban court.

In order to avoid unnecessary repetition, the main findings will only be recapitulated briefly. The persons who were remanded in custody included significantly greater proportions of those charged with breaking and entering offences, of those with criminal records (especially if they had served a custodial sentence), of persons having offences taken into consideration at sentence, and of those who were unemployed (or had held their present job for a very short time), living in lodgings, or of 'no fixed abode'. The importance of breaking and entering offences was not diminished when various aspects of the police inquiries surrounding each offence were taken into account, although the difference between this offence group and the other groups was not as marked when the criminal record and the previous custodial experience of persons in each offence group was taken into account. On the other hand, the persons who were released on bail included a greater proportion of those with no previous criminal record, those facing charges of less serious types of wounding and larceny (especially of property under the value of £10), having been in regular employment for several months, and of those who were living with dependants or relatives.

If these differentiating characteristics are considered in the light of the most frequent types of police objections to bail (see Chapter 5), the main feature which they have in common is the significance of the accused's criminal record. The importance of breaking and entering offences, and the various aspects of a person's 'community ties', which distinguished those in custody from those on bail, did not feature so significantly in police objections to bail; on the other hand, the most frequent type of police objection to bail centred round the likely hampering of police inquiries, and although it was difficult to obtain objective measurements of this from the documentary sources, yet a certain amount of corroboration was found in the evidence concerning other suspects to be traced, further charges to be preferred, and, particularly, other offences taken into consideration.

It may be thought necessary to attempt to reconcile these rather different types of evidence. On the occasions when the police specifically objected to bail on the grounds of the nature of the offence, it was invariably because of the seriousness of an offence of violence against the person; very rarely did they object on the grounds that it was an offence of breaking and entering; however, because of the association that was found between breaking and entering offences and previous criminal record, it may well have been that the police used the criminal record as their main objection to bail in cases of breaking and entering. The police did not object to bail on grounds of the defendant's lack of community ties as often as might have seemed likely, after considering the social characteristics of those remanded in custody; a rather tentative suggestion would be that many of the persons for whom the police objected to bail on grounds of criminal record and likely hampering of police inquiries may well have been persons who were unemployed, living in lodgings, or with no responsibilities towards any dependants. Much of this is clearly very speculative, and it would need a larger research project to confirm or refute the various possible interpretations.

When comparisons were made between the characteristics of persons at the urban and the rural courts, to see if there were any differences which might explain why more were remanded in custody in the urban sample, it was found that in several respects the urban and rural cases were very similar: for example, both groups had approximately the same proportion of persons unemployed, the value of stolen property in offences of larceny and breaking and entering was the same, and the number of offences t.i.c. was similar in the urban and rural cases. When certain other factors were taken into account, the difference between the two groups was not as great; for example, when offence Groups A and B were considered alone, the difference in the proportion remanded in custody was reduced by half; when persons with no criminal record were considered alone, all the courts remanded the same proportion in custody.

The differences that were found in the characteristics of the urban and rural cases usually had no effect upon the different proportions remanded in custody, and the only factors which may have contributed towards this included (i) the majority of cases in which there were other offenders to trace were at the urban court, (ii) more of the persons at the urban court who had previous convictions had also served custodial sentences, and (iii) the urban cases included more single persons living in lodgings. Nevertheless, the urban court still remanded significantly more in custody of persons charged with breaking and entering (Group C), persons with criminal records, and those who were unemployed.

One of the criticisms that can be levelled against the type of analysis carried out in this chapter, is that the association of each factor with the likelihood of being remanded in custody has usually been examined on its own, as if its effect was likely to be independent of the other characteristics in any particular case, thereby ignoring the fact that it may not be the incidence of single factors in isolation which is important in a decision-making process of this kind, but the way in which different factors occur together in each case[1].

The investigations into the association between various aspects of the nature of the different offences and the relationship between offence groups and the previous criminal record, went some way towards meeting this type of criticism; and, although a sophisticated analysis was not possible within the scope of this research project, yet a simple method of scoring the accumulation of different social factors in each case was available from the Vera Foundation's work in the Manhattan Bail Project. The details of the application of this

1. See the relevant discussion, in connection with sentencing decisions, by R. F. Sparks, 'Sentencing by Magistrates', in P. Halmos (Ed.), *Sociological Studies in the British Penal Services*, (Keele, 1965) pp. 71 ff.

scoring method to the present sample will be presented in Chapter 7, but, to anticipate those of the findings which are relevant to the present discussion, it was found that the persons released on bail had double the average score (mainly reflecting the strength of their 'community ties') of those remanded in custody, both in the urban and the rural cases, and in each of the main offence groups. There was no significant difference between the urban scores and the rural scores, confirming the findings of the single-factor analysis, and there remained the consistent pattern whereby the urban court remanded in custody about 10 per cent more of the 'equivalent' cases than the rural courts. Finally, comparing equivalent score cases in each offence group, the urban court still remanded more of the persons in Group C in custody, charged with breaking and entering, although in the rural courts there was no significant difference between the offence groups.

From all the evidence that has been presented, it seems to have been clearly shown that the persons who were remanded in custody at the urban and rural courts had, as a group, many characteristics which distinguished them from those released on bail, that the urban court remanded in custody at least 10 per cent more of comparable cases than the rural cases, and that persons charged with breaking and entering were more likely to be remanded in custody than other offenders, even though their criminal records and custodial experience went some way towards accounting for this tendency.

7. TOWARDS A MANHATTAN BAIL PROJECT IN ENGLAND?

The initiation of the research project, of which the main findings are described in this report, was itself a symptom of the growing interest in the problem of persons remanded in custody before trial, both in this country and, more especially, in the United States of America, where the more obvious shortcomings of their bail system resulted in the pioneering work of the Vera Foundation (now the Vera Institute of Justice, New York) in developing the Manhattan Bail Project[1]. Towards the end of the actual period of research, there were two important developments which provide useful focuses for the discussion, in these two final chapters, of certain conclusions to be drawn from the results of the research. These developments were, firstly, the passing of the Criminal Justice Act, 1967, which included certain provisions for new restrictions upon the refusal of bail (ss. 18–23), and, secondly, plans for the introduction into England of a pilot scheme along similar lines to the Manhattan Bail Project[2].

At the end of Chapter 6, it was mentioned that the scoring system used in the Manhattan Bail Project provided a useful way of examining the extent to which various social characteristics were present together in the cases that were remanded on bail or in custody; and it is also possible to use the scores of the research sample as an indirect opportunity for examining the extent to which a slightly modified application of the scoring techniques used in the Manhattan Bail Project might have affected the magistrates' decisions in these particular remand cases.

This chapter will present the findings of an application of a scoring system, modified from the Manhattan Bail Project, to the present research sample, and Chapter 8 will put forward certain

1. For further details of the Manhattan Bail Project see: C. E. Ares, A. Rankin and H. Sturz, 'The Manhattan Bail Project', 38 *N.Y.U.L.Rev.* 67 (1963); D. J. Freed and P. M. Wald, *Bail in the United States: 1964*, (Washington D.C. 1964) Ch. VI; and M. Zander, 'Bail: A Reappraisal (Part III) [1967] *Crim. L.R.* 128.
2. This pilot scheme is under the direction of Michael Zander, of the London School of Economics; see M. Zander, 'Bail: A Reappraisal' [1967] *Crim. L.R.* 25,100 128; see also C. Davies, 'Imprisonment before Sentence', (Unpublished M.A. thesis, University of Liverpool, 1968) esp. Ch. 5.

proposals for improvement in procedure, in the light of the Criminal Justice Act, 1967.

Application of the scoring system

For the Manhattan Bail Project the Vera Foundation developed a system whereby each defendant was interviewed before appearing in court, and information was obtained about his background, in the following categories: (i) prior record, (ii) family ties, (iii) employment, (iv) residence, (v) time in area, and (vi) a discretionary category including pregnancy, old age, and poor health. A scoring system was devised for each category, and if the defendant had an address in the area, where he could be contacted, and obtained a total score of five points or more, he was considered suitable to be recommended for release on bail.

The slightly modified scoring system, which was applied to the present sample was as follows:

Factor	Score
Prior Record	
No indictable convictions	+2
One indictable conviction	+1
Two indictable convictions	0
Three or more indictable convictions	−1
Family Ties	
Lives with family	+2
Lives with non-family person	+1
Employment	
Present job held for 12 months or more	+3
Present job held for 4 ∠ 12 months	+2
Employed ∠ 4 months, or on sickness benefit	+1
Residence	
Present residence 12 months or more	+3
Present residence 6 ∠ 12 months	+2
Present residence 4 ∠ 6 months	+1
Time in area	
10 years or more	+1
Discretion	
Female, or aged 50 years or more	+1

The total score derived from these categories will be referred to as the 'V'-score, and as all the information was obtained from documentary sources it was treated as verified. Not all the files contained enough information for calculating a full score, so that where it was not possible to assign a score in more than one of the six categories the case was excluded from this analysis. In fact, enough information was available in almost 90 per cent of all cases. When the mean 'V'-scores were calculated (Table 26), the most striking finding was the way in which the bail and custody cases were differentiated: the mean score for bail cases was 7.6, for custody cases 2.9, and for cases which were partly on bail and partly in custody exactly 5.0.

TABLE 26

'V'-scores of persons remanded on bail and in custody, in each offence group: Urban and Rural Courts, 1963–65

Offence group	TOTAL		Bail		Custody		Bail & Custody	
	Mean score	(no.)	Mean score	(no.)	Mean score	(no.)	Mean score	(no.)
URBAN COURT								
A (Violence)	6·3	(50)	8·2	(23)	4·2	(18)	5·7	(9)
B (Larcenies)	5·5	(264)	7·7	(112)	3·4	(108)	5·6	(44)
C (Breakings)	3·3	(284)	8·1	(32)	2·6	(232)	4·0	(20)
Total	4·5	(598)	7·8	(167)	2·9	(358)	5·1	(73)
RURAL COURTS								
A (Violence)	4·5	(11)	6·7	(6)	1·0	(3)	3·5	(2)
B (Larcenies)	5·1	(102)	7·5	(45)	2·7	(51)	6·8	(6)
C (Breakings)	3·8	(68)	5·0	(17)	3·1	(36)	3·9	(15)
Total	4·6	(181)	6·8	(68)	2·8	(90)	4·6	(23)
ALL CASES								
A (Violence)	6·0	(61)	7·9	(29)	3·7	(21)	5·3	(11)
B (Larcenies)	5·4	(366)	7·6	(157)	3·2	(159)	5·6	(50)
C (Breakings)	3·4	(352)	7·1	(49)	2·6	(268)	3·9	(35)
Grand Total	4·5	(779)	7·6	(235)	2·9	(448)	5·0	(96)

As the nature of the offence is not included as an element in calculating the score, a comparison of the scores in each offence group will show the extent to which each group included persons with different background characteristics. The mean scores of all cases in each of the Groups A, B and C was 6.0, 5.4 and 3.4, respectively; these ratios correspond closely to the relative proportions released on bail. Within each offence group, in both the urban and the rural courts, there was a marked difference in the scores of those released on bail and those remanded in custody; however, at the urban court, there was no difference in the mean scores of those granted bail in each of the offence groups, and, at the rural courts, of all those remanded in custody, Group C (Breaking and Entering) had the *highest* average score.

In the experimental group of the Manhattan Bail Project, a person was considered suitable for release on bail if he obtained a total score of at least five points. Thus an alternative way of examining the application of the Vera system was to divide the cases into those scoring above and below the critical total of five points. The results of this exercise are shown in Tables 27 and 28.

In the total sample, exactly half scored less than five points (Table 27); only 7 per cent of these were always granted bail, and as many as 80 per cent were remanded in custody all the time before their trial. Fourteen per cent of the rural cases scoring less than five points were released on bail, compared to less than 6 per cent of the urban, which confirms the finding of the previous chapter, that the urban court remanded rather more persons, with comparable characteristics, in custody than did the rural courts. Comparing the different offence groups, the urban court remanded more equivalent cases in custody from Group C than the other offence groups (statistically significant), but in the rural courts a greater proportion of equivalent cases were remanded in custody from Group B than from Group C.

TABLE 27

Percentage of persons with 'V'–scores of less than 5, remanded on bail and in custody, in each offence group

Offence group	TOTAL no.	(%)*	Bail %	Custody %	Bail & Custody %
URBAN COURT					
A (Violence)	11	(22·0)	9·1	72·7	18·2
B (Larcenies)	104	(39·4)	11·5	69·3	19·2
C (Breakings)	188	(66·2)	2·1	89·4	8·5
Total	303	(50·6)	5·6	81·9	12·5
RURAL COURTS					
A (Violence)	5	(45·5)	20·0	60·0	20·0
B (Larcenies)	42	(41·2)	14·3	83·3	2·4
C (Breakings)	39	(57·4)	12·8	64·1	23·1
Total	86	(47·5)	14·0	73·2	12·8
ALL CASES					
A (Violence)	16	(26·2)	12·5	68·7	18·8
B (Larcenies)	146	(39·9)	12·3	73·3	14·4
C (Breakings)	227	(64·5)	4·0	85·0	11·0
Grand Total	389	(50·0)	7·4	80·0	12·6

*Expresses the number of cases as a percentage of the total number in each category for which a score could be calculated.

Tests of significance: Groups A and B compared with Group C:

(i) Urban Court: $chi^2 = 11{\cdot}8$ (P ∠ 0·001)
(ii) Rural Courts: $chi^2 = 0{\cdot}2$ (n.s.)
(iii) All cases: $chi^2 = 9{\cdot}3$ (P ∠ 0·005)

The remaining half of the sample scored five or more points (Table 28); 35 per cent of these cases were remanded in custody on every occasion, and only just over half of them were always released on bail. Once again, the urban court remanded more in custody than the rural courts 37 per cent, compared to 28 per cent. Using this criterion, of a score of five or more points, for comparing the offence groups, it was found that a significantly greater proportion in Group C were remanded in custody at the urban court, although the differences between the offence groups at the rural courts did not reach statistical significance.

TABLE 28

Percentage of persons with 'V-scores of 5 or more, remanded on bail and in custody, in each offence group.

Offence group	TOTAL no.	(%)*	Bail %	Custody %	Bail & Custody %
URBAN COURT					
A (Violence)	39	(78·0)	56·4	25·7	17·9
B (Larcenies)	160	(60·6)	62·5	22·5	15·0
C (Breakings)	96	(33·8)	28·1	66·7	4·2
Total	295	(49·4)	50·9	37·3	11·8
RURAL COURTS					
A (Violence)	6	(54·5)	83·3	—	16·7
B (Larcenies)	60	(58·8)	65·0	26·7	8·3
C (Breakings)	29	(42·6)	41·4	37·9	20·7
Total	95	(52·5)	59·0	28·4	12·6
ALL CASES					
A (Violence)	45	(73·8)	60·0	22·2	17·8
B (Larcenies)	220	(60·1)	63·2	23·6	13·2
C (Breakings)	125	(35·5)	32·0	60·0	8·0
Grand Total	390	(50·0)	52·8	35·2	12·0

*Expresses the number of cases as a percentage of the total number of cases in each category for which a score could be calculated.

Tests of significance: Groups A and B compared with Group C:

(i) Urban Court: $chi^2 = 42{\cdot}8$ ($P \angle 0{\cdot}001$)
(ii) Rural Courts: $chi^2 = 2{\cdot}5$ (n.s.)
(iii) All cases: $chi^2 = 44{\cdot}5$ ($P \angle 0{\cdot}001$)

This application of the Vera scoring system has confirmed the results of the single-factor analysis presented in Chapter 6. The persons released on bail had double the average score of those remanded in custody; this applied to both urban and rural cases, and to cases within each offence group. The urban and rural samples had very similar background characteristics, as far as was reflected by the 'V' score, and the urban court consistently remanded more equivalent cases in custody than the rural courts. Finally, persons in the main offence groups had different average scores, roughly corresponding to the different proportions remanded in custody; but, comparing equivalent cases in each group, the urban court still remanded more of those charged with breaking and entering offences (Group C) in custody.

The other main conclusion to be drawn from this retrospective application of the Vera scoring system is that if such a system had been used *in advance* to determine the magistrates' decisions in these cases (as in the Manhattan Project), this would have meant that more than a third of those remanded in custody all the time would have been released on bail, and 7 per cent of those released on bail would have been remanded in custody.

In his recent application of the Manhattan Bail Project scores to a group of young Liverpool men, charged with breaking and entering offences, Clive Davies (1968) found that as many as 77 per cent of his sample, who were in custody all the time from arrest until sentence, would have scored five or more points, indicating suitability for release according to these criteria. Although this figure seems to be very high, yet it is similar to that of those charged with breaking and entering offences (Group C) at the urban court, where 67 per cent of those in custody all the time scored five or more. (Table 28). In contrast to Group C, less than a quarter of all persons remanded in custody in Groups A and B scored five or more points. It seems probable that specific circumstances apply to cases involving breaking and entering offenders; these special considerations, almost certainly connected with previous criminal records and police inquiries, seemed to have outweighed the social and community factors which are the main elements contributing to the Vera scores.

Possible implications

On the basis of the evidence from these two studies, it can almost certainly be assumed, in general terms, that a majority of persons charged with breaking and entering offences in urban areas, who are remanded in custody, would obtain a 'pass' score, if a Manhattan Bail Project scheme were to be applied in this country; and even in the case of persons charged with other indictable offences, a significant proportion would also obtain a 'pass' score. There will, however, be differences of opinion about the implications of these findings.

It has been rightly pointed out by Michael Zander that the main concern of the approach adopted in the Manhattan Bail Project was with criteria thought to be directly related to the question of likely appearance at trial, and that this approach reflected the major emphasis in the American system of bail determination (Zander, 1967). In practice, virtually all these criteria simply reflect the 'community ties' of a person (with the exception of the score for criminal record). In the English system, however, not only can other factors properly be considered by magistrates as indirectly affecting the risk of absconding, but observation in the urban and rural courts showed that police objections to bail frequently included the risk that the course of justice might be impeded, either by witnesses being threatened or police inquiries hampered in other ways, and the possibility of a repetition of the offence or similar offences, if the defendant were to be released on bail; factors which might be relevant to the possible repetition of the offence include the nature and seriousness of the offence, the defendant's previous criminal record, or the fact that offences had been previously committed on bail.

For a scheme like that in Manhattan to be at all realistic for this country, it would seem to be necessary to incorporate information relevant to these additional aspects into the scoring calculations; unfortunately, by its very nature, this kind of information is not only more difficult to obtain but it is also difficult to convert into numerical terms. Nevertheless, there are many attractions in attempting to adapt the Manhattan system for our own needs; magistrates would be able to base their decisions on much more information than at present, and it would be information which had been independently verified; there would be a regular interview or questionnaire schedule used throughout the country, encouraging a greater standardization of procedure in bail decisions; and magistrates would always have basic information in the light of which to consider police objections or defence applications for bail. The main feature which it does not seem feasible to adopt in England is the points system, and as this scoring system provides the basis for the whole procedure, to reject that part might appear to be a rejection of the whole system.

Several considerations have led to what may seem to be a rather pessimistic and defeatist conclusion. It would appear to be a virtually impossible task to calculate a satisfactory points-weighting for information about the likely repetition of offences, threats to witnesses and the hampering of police enquiries; and even if a way was found of incorporating these factors into the scoring system, magistrates are not likely to welcome this kind of 'aid' to their decision-making, whereby they would feel to have lost their traditional independence and have become merely mouthpieces for announcing the result of an impersonal statistical calculation.

The main objection is one which questions the fundamental validity of this kind of 'prediction' for decisions about bail. A points system, like that developed by the Vera Foundation, is essentially claiming to be a prediction instrument; it predicts that there is only a minimal risk, if any, that a person who scores five or more points will not appear for his trial if released on bail. However, the usual way of devising a prediction instrument is by basing it on a past sample of persons whose particular behaviour (which the research worker wants eventually to be able to predict) has or has not already occurred; in the present context, this would have involved following up a group of defendants who had *all* been released on bail, and basing the prediction score on a comparison between those who appeared for trial and those who absconded. This complicated procedure was not used initially by the Vera Foundation, and perhaps it could not have been expected, because of the inevitable risks involved; instead, it is assumed that the weighting system for each factor and the 'cut-off' score were arbitrarily assigned in the first place, and then subjected to experimental practice of a kind, in the pilot study of the Manhattan Bail Project[1]. Its validity was 'confirmed' by the apparent success of the Manhattan Project and the many other projects that followed in the United States. If it is intended to introduce a similar scheme into this country, where many of the problems and relevant circumstances appear to be quite different from those obtaining in the United States, all that can be expected is a similar unsophisticated process of trial and error, which may or may not be successful. An added complication is that the success of any such pilot scheme would be difficult to assess, in terms of the factors which are of concern to English courts and the police, and which are considered relevant to the bail decision.

The underlying assumptions and intentions behind an English pilot scheme are of obvious importance in determining the methods adopted. If a new scoring system were to be devised which accurately distinguished those *currently* remanded in custody from those on bail, its application would only succeed in maintaining the *status quo*, or at most standardizing it according to practice in a particular area or type of court. If, on the other hand, it is thought that an unnecessarily large proportion of persons are being remanded in custody, the scoring system could be adjusted in order to ensure that more persons were released on bail. There would inevitably be so much uncertainty and guesswork involved in such a procedure, that it would seem a waste of effort to try to devise a system for basing bail decisions on a scientific precision, which cannot be achieved. It would certainly be valuable to develop a national system for the collection of regular information about all the defendants appearing on remand, but without going to the more extreme lengths of trying to emulate the Manhattan Project's scoring system, revised in the light of the English situation and experience.

Ideally, this information ought to be collected by an independent agency; in the United States most Bail Projects utilize the services of Law Students or the Probation Department. Similarly, perhaps, in England the Probation Service might seem to be the natural choice for such a new assignment, but it is doubtful whether they

1. This interpretation receives confirmation from correspondence between H. Sturz (of the Vera Institute) and Clive Davies, see C. Davies (1968) p. 131.

would welcome this addition to their already heavy workload, particularly as it would be a fairly routine fact-finding procedure, not requiring the professional skills of their officers. The most practical solution, involving a certain degree of compromise with the ideal of an independent agency, would be for the schedule to be completed by the police; much of the information would already be in their possession, and in most cases the police have eventually to produce an 'antecedents' report for the court. There could still be opportunities for both sides to put forward additional reasons in court, as to why bail should or should not be granted, but if the magistrates were initially provided with a comprehensive survey of the basic facts they would be in a far better position to judge the merits of each case, and to exercise their discretion in a more meaningful way.

8. CONCLUSIONS: CRIMINAL JUSTICE ACT, 1967, AND BEYOND

Clarification of principles

As the field-work for the research progressed, during 1965 and 1966, it became clear to the author that magistrates ought to have had more guidance on the general principles to be applied in dealing with remand decisions before trial. What guidance there was in law, at that time, seemed to place too great an emphasis on the question of appearance at trial, while ignoring many other considerations that were equally or more important in practice. Subsequent analysis of the content of police objections to bail led to the conclusion that there ought to be at least three general principles which could justify the refusal of bail, namely:

(i) The risk of non-appearance at trial.
(ii) The likelihood of a repetition of the offence or similar offences.
(iii) Evidence that the course of justice might be impeded.

If there seemed to be sound evidence for any of these risks being present in a case before them, magistrates would be justified in remanding the defendant in custody. Depending on the form in which these principles were presented for the guidance of magistrates, there could be a discussion of each general principle, with a list of specific factors and circumstances likely to be relevant; such a list would be intended for guidance only, and not to be regarded as completely exhaustive of all possible relevant factors. It will be seen (below) that the Criminal Justice Act, 1967, can be criticized for attempting to draw up a complete list of specific circumstances in which the restrictions on the refusal of bail need not apply, instead of stating more general principles for the guidance of the courts; it is impossible to foresee every likely circumstance that might arise, and it would seem to be more satisfactory to leave a certain amount of interpretation to the discretion of the magistrates.

On the basis of the present research findings, the following factors would provide initial guidance for the interpretation of the three suggested principles:

(i) *The risk of non-appearance at trial*: e.g. lack of community ties, nature and seriousness of the offence, the strength of the prosecution evidence, and the likelihood of conviction.
(ii) *The likelihood of a repetition of the offence:* e.g. nature and seriousness of the offence, defendant's previous criminal record, and offences committed on bail.
(iii) *Evidence that the course of justice might be impeded:* e.g. nature and extent of further police inquiries, likely threats to witnesses.

As a corollary to these proposals, when the magistrates have reached a decision to remand a person in custody, they should be required to state for which of the three main reasons they have refused bail, and the evidence upon which they have reached their decision[1]. It is hoped that this requirement would achieve several objects: it would serve to direct the attention of the magistrates more closely to a consideration of the reasons for refusing bail; it would provide guidance for the police; it seems right that each defendant should know the reason for being kept in custody; and it may be of some assistance to him if he decides to apply for bail to a Judge in Chambers.

The Criminal Justice Act, 1967, was passed at the end of the period covered by this research, and its provisions for the restriction of the refusal of bail (ss. 18–23) came into operation on 1st January, 1968. The provisions are complicated, with regard to the cases in which they are applicable, but the main points can be summarized. Except in a list of defined circumstances, magistrates' courts can no longer refuse bail to persons (over the age of 17) charged with offences which are punishable on summary conviction by not more than six months imprisonment; if the offence is an indictable offence, triable summarily, the court must have commenced to hear it summarily (by s. 18 or s. 19 of the Magistrates' Courts Act, 1952), which means that the magistrates still have discretionary power to remand in custody *before a plea* has been taken in such an offence. Also, in a summary offence, where the prosecutor or the accused claims jury trial (s. 25 of the M.C.A. 1952), the committal for trial must be on bail, unless any of the defined circumstances obtain.

There are eight defined circumstances under which a court can remand in custody, in those cases which otherwise would be on bail:

(i) where the offence is punishable for a term of not less than six months, and the person has been previously sentenced to imprisonment or borstal;

1. The Criminal Justice Act, 1967, s.18(8) requires magistrates to give written notice of reasons for refusal of bail, but only when committing for trial legally unrepresented defendants.

(ii) where he has previously failed to comply with the conditions of any recognisance for release on bail;
(iii) where he is charged with an offence alleged to have been committed on bail;
(iv) where it is necessary to detain him to establish his identity or address;
(v) where he has no fixed abode, or is ordinarily resident outside the United Kingdom;
(vi) where the offence charged involves an assault on or threat of violence to another person, or involves firearms or explosives, or is one of indecent conduct with or towards a person under 16;
(vii) where he is likely to commit an offence if granted bail;
(viii) where it is necessary for his own protection to detain him in custody.

Bail can also be refused if the defendant fails to enter into proper recognisances or to provide satisfactory sureties if required.

The existence of any one of these circumstances does not mean that magistrates must then automatically *refuse* bail, but, as Napley (1967) has pointed out, the setting down of these specific factors may result in the refusal of bail *wherever* they apply, and also in their application to cases in which the decision to release on bail is still discretionary. In fact, the statistics for 1968, recently published in the *Report on the Work of the Prison Department, 1968: Statistical Tables* (Home Office, 1970), show that magistrates' courts still remanded more in custody in 1968 than in 1967, of persons tried summarily, although a smaller proportion of those committed for trial to higher courts were committed in custody.

Many of the circumstances, defined in the Criminal Justice Act, appeared in the police objections to bail at the observed courts, and many of them were characteristics which distinguished those in the sample who were remanded in custody, from those on bail; but the final form of the Act did not have adequate provision for cases where the police feared that their further inquiries would be hindered, and it failed to give general guidance about the underlying justification for particular reasons for the refusal of bail.

Improvements in procedure

1. *Legal representation.*

During the periods of observation at the urban and rural courts, exactly half of the persons who were remanded in custody by the magistrates had not made any application for bail (Table 7, above); twenty-two defendants, who were not legally represented, applied for bail in the face of police objections, and two (9 per cent) were successful; of the twenty-six defendants who were represented and applied for bail, against police objections, five (19 per cent) were successful. Zander (1967) found that 'whereas 20 per cent of the sixty-six unrepresented bail applicants were successful, 41 per cent of the twenty-seven who were represented succeeded in the face of police objections' (p. 109). We have also seen that more information was provided in cases where the defendant was legally represented, especially about the defendant's 'community ties'.

These observations draw attention to the need for ensuring that defendants are fully aware of their right to apply for bail, and suggest that closer attention should be paid to the question of obtaining legal representation at the earliest opportunity, so that a defendant can be represented when applying for bail.

It was possible to investigate the extent of legal representation among the 203 remand cases at the urban court, during 1964 (Table 29). In cases tried summarily, 11 per cent were represented as early as

TABLE 29

Legal representation and the granting of bail: Urban Court, 1964

	TOTAL		Bail		Custody		Bail & Custody	
	no.	(%)	no.	(%)	no.	(%)	no.	(%)
Tried summarily								
Represented, remand and trial	16	(10·8)	10	(62·5)	2	(12·5)	4	(25·0)
Represented, trial only	28	(18·9)	16	(57·2)	9	(32·1)	3	(10·7)
Never represented	104	(70·3)	28	(26·9)	66	(63·5)	10	(9·6)
Total	148	(100·0)	54	(36·5)	77	(52·0)	17	(11·5)
Tried at higher court								
Represented, remand and trial	7	(12·7)	1	(14·3)	5	(71·4)	1	(14·3)
Represented, trial only	34	(61·8)	10	(29·4)	15	(44·1)	9	(26·5)
Never represented	14	(25·5)	2	(14·3)	12	(85·7)	—	—
Total	55	(100·0)	13	(23·6)	32	(58·2)	10	(18·2)
All cases								
Represented, remand and trial	23	(11·3)	11	(47·9)	7	(30·4)	5	(21·7)
Represented, trial only	62	(30·5)	26	(41·9)	24	(38·7)	12	(19·4)
Never represented	118	(58·2)	30	(25·4)	78	(66·1)	10	(8·5)
Grand Total	203	(100·0)	67	(33·0)	109	(53·7)	27	(13·3)

Tests of significance: A. Those represented at trial *and* remand, compared with those never represented:
(i) tried summarily: $chi^2 = 11·0$ ($P \angle 0·001$)
(ii) tried at higher court: $chi^2 = 0·1$ (n.s.)
(iii) all cases: $chi^2 = 6·4$ ($P \angle 0·025$)

B. Those represented *only at trial*, compared with those never represented:
(i) tried summarily: $chi^2 = 8·0$ ($P \angle 0·005$)
(ii) tried at higher court: $chi^2 = 0·2$ (n.s.)
(iii) all cases: $chi^2 = 7·7$ ($P \angle 0·01$)

the remand hearing, with a further 19 per cent represented at their trial; 70 per cent were not represented at any time. As many as 62 per cent of those legally represented at the remand hearing were granted bail, with only 12 per cent always remanded in custody; but, of those who were not represented at any time, only 27 per cent were granted bail, and 63 per cent were always remanded in custody.

Although these figures are significant, there are indications that the greater frequency of bail might be explained by the difference in the type of case which was legally represented, rather than in terms of direct cause and effect of being represented; this possibility is indicated by the fact that as many as 57 per cent of persons *not represented until trial* had been granted bail for all the pre-trial period.

In the smaller number of cases tried at a higher court, exactly the same proportion of persons represented on remand were granted bail as of those not represented at all (14 per cent); but as many as 29 per cent of persons represented only at their trial had been granted bail. This again points in the direction of an interpretation in terms of an *association* between the type of case in which bail was granted and the type which was likely to be legally represented, rather than a *causal* connection between legal representation and release on bail.

Nevertheless, it is important that when the police ask for a remand in custody, the defendant should be told in clear terms that he can, if he so wishes, apply for bail; and it ought to be possible for legal aid to be available so that a solicitor can make an application for bail, even if a person does not wish to be legally represented at his trial. The Widgery Committee (1966) on Legal Aid in Criminal Proceedings rejected the suggestion that legal aid, granted to an accused person for the preparation and conduct of his defence, should extend to applications for bail, whether at magistrates' courts or to a Judge in Chambers; but the Committee did make some other important recommendations about facilities for persons in custody (either of the police or prison authorities) to be made fully aware of their rights to legal aid and advice. These recommendations are particularly important in the present context, because a person usually comes into the custody of the police before he appears in court, and if a request for a solicitor is delayed until the actual court appearance this results either in a very hurried briefing of a solicitor on his behalf or a further short period in police custody.

Whatever the correct interpretation of the statistics concerning legal representation and bail, and even if the courts were to be eventually provided with standardized information about each defendant, there would still seem to be a *prima facie* need in certain cases for a defendant's application for bail to be put to the court by a solicitor, and in these circumstances it is right that legal aid should be available for this part of the proceedings irrespective of whether legal aid is required for any of the later stages.

2. *Prejudicial material*

An acceptance of the need for comprehensive information, about a person who is being remanded before trial, would accentuate certain problems about prejudicial material which exist to a lesser degree already. The main kinds of information which are considered potentially prejudicial to an accused person are details of his previous criminal record, and allegations about the offence with which he is charged. Prejudice could be created in the minds of the magistrates, and also among members of the public who attend the court or read an account of the hearing in the local press. As far as concerns details of a person's criminal record, the Criminal Justice Act, 1967, (s.19.1), made a bold attempt to solve this problem by ruling that a magistrate should not adjudicate at the summary trial or committal proceedings of an accused person if, in the course of proceedings for the determination of bail, he has been informed that the person has any previous convictions. This new ruling may either result in direct evidence of the accused's previous criminal record being put forward by the police in fewer cases than at present, or alternatively may create considerable administrative difficulties to ensure that the trial magistrates have not been involved in a remand hearing at which previous convictions were disclosed. This provision does not cover any other prejudicial material besides criminal record, but this would be much more difficult to specify.

The other aspect of this problem, that of press publicity of information revealed at remand hearings, was also tackled by the Criminal Justice Act. Before the passing of the Act, the press were usually cooperative in not publishing any details of previous convictions, at the request of the magistrates, but in cases of local or national importance it was usual to report full details of other police allegations about the offence, supporting their request for a remand in custody. The main concern of the Criminal Justice Act, 1967, in this respect, was to restrict the reporting of *committal proceedings* (ss. 3–6), normally allowing only the names of persons involved, the actual offence charged, and the court decision to be published; but it was made clear, by the definitions in ss. 35–36, that these reporting restrictions apply to all the earlier stages of indictable offences, except when (or until) a court has decided to deal with it summarily. In practice, therefore, this means that the reporting of the earlier remand hearings of all indictable offences is restricted, except when it has been decided to try the cases summarily. In any of these circumstances, it is still open to the defendant to request that full publicity be given.

There seems no good reason why similar restrictions should not apply to the reporting of all remand hearings, and not just to those nevertheless, the new restrictions mark an important step forward, involving indictable offences which might be tried at a higher court;

and the only other interim proposal would be that in exceptional cases, not covered by these new restrictions, it should be possible for the prosecution or defence to make an application for a particular hearing to be held *in camera*, to enable details of the alleged offence or of the accused's criminal record to be given without any fear of prejudicial publicity (see 'Justice', 1966, §18).

3. *Conditions of bail*

Before the 1st January, 1968, no conditions which magistrates might impose upon a defendant, whom they released on bail, had any legal validity as such. This did not mean that magistrates never imposed any conditions of bail, but only that if there was a breach of the conditions the police could not rearrest the defendant on those grounds alone. In practice, one of the most common conditions was for the accused to be asked to surrender his passport, and with this condition no 'breach' could occur once the passport was in the hands of the police.

When s. 21 of the Criminal Justice Act came into operation at the beginning of 1968, any court releasing a person on bail was given a wide discretion to impose any conditions 'likely to result in his appearance at the time and place required, or to be necessary in the interests of justice or for the prevention of crime'. This particular section of the Act was added only during the Committee Stage of the Bill, as a direct result of the *Interim Report on Bail and Remands in Custody*, published in December, 1966, by the 'Justice' Working Party, which gave some examples of the kind of conditions envisaged:

> Such conditions could relate to such matters as residence, regular reporting to the police, restrictions on travel by surrender of passport, disconnection of telephone, and an undertaking not to interfere with witnesses. Legislation ought not to particularize conditions, even by way of example, because it is impossible statutorily to provide for every case that might arise.
>
> ('Justice', 1966, § 10)

Although a court cannot require sureties for the performance of any extra condition imposed, other than the attendance of the accused at trial (s.21.2), if a condition is not observed the police are now empowered to rearrest the person (s.23.1).

If this new provision results in persons being released on *conditional* bail, who before might have been remanded in custody, it will serve a useful purpose—assuming these persons turn out to be 'good risk's; on the other hand, extra conditions are unlikely to deter the person who is determined to abscond or in any other way interfere with the course of justice, and the new powers of rearrest are not likely to be very successful in these circumstances, as the damage will have already been done. Nevertheless, on the balance of probabilities, it seems more likely to result in the release of persons for whom custody is unnecessary, rather than being abused by the majority of persons who are so released.

4. *Applications for bail to a Judge in Chambers*

The only remedy or form of appeal, against a refusal of bail by a magistrates' court, lies in applying for bail to a Judge in Chambers. No regular statistics are published of these applications, but in 1956 there was a total of 1,665, of which 7 per cent were granted (Devlin, 1960); by 1966 the number of applications had risen to as many as 3,885, of which 281 (7.3 per cent) were granted[1].

In the sample of 416 remand cases, there were 19 known cases of applications to a Judge in Chambers, which was slightly more than 7 per cent of the total of 263 persons who spent some time in custody. None of the applications was directly successful: in thirteen cases the application was immediately turned down, and in the remaining six cases, the decision was postponed to await the outcome of the applicant's next appearance in court (usually committal proceedings), when, without exception, the magistrates released them all on bail.

The Official Solicitor normally acts on behalf of the applicant, in presenting his application to the Judge, and, to assist the Judge's determination of the bail application, information is requested from the local police, under the following heads:

1. Date of arrest.
2. Tribunal committing for trial, and date.
3. Particulars of offence, and date.
4. Date and place of trial.
5. Age of prisoner.
6. Whether a Defence Certificate was granted on committal.
7. Any indication as to plea at trial, or whether he disputed the evidence for the prosecution?
8. Do police object to bail, and, if so, the reasons?
9. Previous convictions.

The applicant is also asked to give the name of persons to act as sureties, and the police are requested to make enquiries as to their suitability and willingness to stand.

Considering all that is involved in being remanded in custody, it may seem surprising that apparently only 7 or 8 per cent of remand prisoners apply to a Judge in Chambers for bail. Several reasons may contribute to this state of affairs: ignorance of the right to apply;

---

1. These most recent figures were kindly supplied to the author by the Official Solicitor; in addition to the cases in which bail was granted by a Judge in Chambers, 'a small number were referred to the current court of trial or bailed by magistrates' (personal communication from the Official Solicitor).

lack of confidence in the claims of their particular case; general scepticism about the chances of an application being successful; and the fact that many are only remanded in custody for a few days, so that even a successful application would not be of much real benefit.

Scepticism about the chances of an application being successful is well grounded in the statistics, which show that only about one out of every fourteen applicants is successful; and the validity of the time factor is always likely to remain, even with an improved system of pre-trial release. The main factors which could be remedied are the remand prisoners' ignorance of the right to apply to a Judge in Chambers, and the general lack of encouragement to make such an application. Routine information about applying is given to every person received into prison on remand, but it would seem that a greater effort could be made to communicate it to the prisoner in a similar way to that recommended by the Widgery Committee (1966) for information about legal aid; the written information could be supplemented by personal discussion with a reception officer designated to deal with such questions as legal aid and bail applications. There is also much to be said in favour of the proposal (incorporated into the Criminal Justice Act, 1967, s. 18.7) that, when magistrates remand a person in custody they should tell him clearly of his right to apply for bail to a Judge in Chambers. These proposals should go some way towards alleviating the apparent finality of the refusal of bail, and, in cases where the defendant is legally represented, will give him an opportunity to discuss the application with his solicitor immediately after the court hearing.

Conclusions

Various reasons have been suggested in recent years for the need for reforming the system whereby English magistrates decide upon the granting or refusal of bail to untried persons. Some of these reasons are of a legal and philosophical nature, in which there is little or no place for evidence collected during research field-work; questions such as whether bail should or should not be regarded as the right of the subject, or what are the implications of the traditional 'presumption of innocence' for persons remanded in custody, certainly ought to be discussed, but they are not questions to which this type of empirical research can provide ready answers.

A second group of reasons, concerning the possible effects of remands in custody upon the outcome of the trial, ought to be reassessed in the light of the present research findings, and at least be regarded as not yet proven. These reasons include the claims that persons remanded in custody are more likely to plead guilty, to be convicted, and to be given a custodial sentence; in all these instances, which are themselves cumulative, the most probable explanation of the statistical correlations is that similar underlying factors are alike responsible for the initial remand in custody and for the subsequent plea, conviction and sentence.

A final group of reasons have a validity which cannot be fundamentally questioned: it is an undeniable fact that being remanded in custody before trial causes considerable hardship and distress, not only for the person immediately concerned, but also for his family; considerable inconvenience (possibly creating inefficiency or injustice) is caused for a solicitor whose client is remanded in custody; and the administrative problems for the prison system of dealing with the rapid turnover of 'remand and trial' prisoners, and arranging escorts from an already overstretched prison staff, cannot be ignored. All these factors must be openly recognized and continual efforts made to alleviate them wherever possible; but in the final analysis, they have to be weighed in the balance against the alternative (and largely unknown) risks that might be involved in releasing more persons on bail before trial.

The main conclusions to which the author has been drawn in the course of his research are, on the one hand, that despite the Criminal Justice Act, there is still need for greater clarification of the principles for which bail can be refused, a need for a standardized system of regular information on persons being remanded, to enable more 'rational' decisions to be taken, and for still more improvements in procedure, particularly to ensure that all accused persons are aware of their rights to apply for bail and that they are given a proper chance to exercise these rights. Yet, on the other hand, there is the further conclusion that, despite these grounds for improvement, most of the decisions taken in the courts were reasonably fair and effective; not only was there a minimal reliance placed upon any financial sanction and careful attention paid to sureties (in the minority of cases where these were considered necessary), but also there was the hint from experience at the rural courts, that, where more defendants were released on bail, there was an increased likelihood of other crimes being committed. It is hoped that this last risk can be minimized by improved selection of cases to be released on bail, and that the various improvements which have been proposed will achieve just such an improved mechanism for selection.

Implementation of the proposals which have been outlined in these last two chapters may or may not increase the proportion of persons who are released on bail, instead of being kept in custody before trial; inasmuch as some of the proposed changes are similar to those included in the Criminal Justice Act, 1967, there will be an opportunity to measure the effect of these by examining any changes after the 1st January, 1968. In fact, first published statistics show that more persons were remanded in custody in 1968 than in 1967, which suggests that the effects of the new provisions have not been as great as was expected. Speculation is never very profitable, and in this context no firm predictions can safely be made. The total effect in numerical terms throughout the country may not be very great; any decrease in the number of persons remanded in custody by some courts may be balanced by an actual increase in other courts. Whatever quantitative changes might occur, there would be a great improvement in the quality of the decisions taken in future, under the new system. Decision-making about bail in magistrates' courts would no longer be the rather haphazard process which all too frequently it is at the moment; the magistrates would still retain their discretion but would exercise it in the light of more relevant information. Policy and practice throughout the country could thus achieve a greater consistency, and it is hoped that a system would emerge in which the right of every individual to personal liberty would be fairly balanced against the right of the state to deprive the individual of that liberty under certain carefully defined circumstances.

APPENDIX METHODOLOGICAL DETAILS

The problems of the initial selection of the courts to be studied in this research have been outlined in the main text. There were no national statistics of the remand practices of magistrates' courts, to provide a sampling frame from which to select a representative sample of courts, or even to use as an indication of how typical was the practice of any courts chosen for study. In these circumstances, it was decided to use the same group of courts, both for the periods of observation and for the drawing of a sample of remanded persons. This Appendix describes in rather more detail (a) the selection of the sample, (b) documentary sources consulted for the sample, and (c) court observation.

Selection of the sample

It was estimated that a total sample of approximately 400 cases could be dealt with in the time available, and at the required depth; half this basic sample was to be drawn from the urban court and half from the rural courts. It was intended to stratify the sample into three main groups of indictable offenders (over the age of seventeen years):

Group A: Violence against the person (non-sexual).
Group B: Larceny and False Pretences.
Group C: Breaking and Entering Offences.

Group A was the most difficult to delineate, because of the great variation in the nature and degree of seriousness of offences of violence (even when excluding sexual offences), and the small numbers which would be included in some categories (e.g. murder, robbery with violence). Ultimately, only the following offences were included

(i) *Felonious Wounding*: wounding with intent to do grievous bodily harm (5.1)*. (Offences against the Person Act, 1861, s. 18)

* The numbers in brackets refer to the classification used by the Home Office in the *Criminal Statistics, England and Wales.*

(ii) *Malicious Wounding*: inflicting grievous bodily harm (8.1) (O.A.P.A. 1861 s. 20)
(iii) *Occasioning actual bodily harm*: (8.6) (O.A.P.A. 1861, s.47)
(iv) *Possessing an offensive weapon*: (8.11)

Group B included all the larcenies and false pretences in Classes III and V of the Home Office Statistical Classification, with the addition of the offence of taking and driving away a motor vehicle without the owner's consent (138). *Group C* included all the breaking and entering offences in Class II (excluding robbery (34) and blackmail (35)).

The registers of the selected courts were examined and a record was made of all the offenders in the three groups, who appeared at these courts during the most recent year (1964), noting whether or not they were remanded. In the urban court it was possible to select the required number of remand cases for each group, by taking a complete sample of Group A for 1964 (57 cases), and a one in four sample of cases in Groups B and C, for the same year, with seventy and seventy-six cases respectively; the total sample from the urban court was thus 203.

The number of indictable offenders appearing before the rural courts in 1964 was only about one-ninth of the number at the urban court. If the period of time was extended to the three years 1963–65, the total number of remand cases reached the 200 mark; unfortunately, there were very few remands in Group A, but instead of attempting to increase the number in Group A, by extending the period as far back as 1955/56, it was decided to make a complete sample of remands from 1963–65: viz. Group A—18 cases; Group B—116; and Group C—79. This gave a total sample of 213 cases from the rural courts.

Because the sampling proportions of Groups B and C were different in the two samples (25 per cent in the urban and 100 per cent in the rural), this meant that in those parts of the analysis which involved comparing the whole urban sample with the whole rural sample, a reweighting calculation had to be carried out so that each offence group would constitute the proper proportion of each sample. This reweighting involved multiplying the urban Groups B and C by four, so that the total reweighted sample at the urban court was: Group A—57 cases; Group B—280; and Group C—304. The reweighted urban total was thus 641 cases.

Documentary sources

Detailed information was collected from the selected remand cases, and recorded on a separate schedule for each offender; this information was later transferred onto punch-cards, facilitating statistical analysis. The information included details of the following:

(a) *Personal details*: age, sex, marital status.
(b) *Family and residence* : dependants, contacts with family, place/time of present residence, and pattern of past residence.
(c) *Employment history.*
(d) *Previous convictions.*
(e) *Present offence* : details of all the circumstances of the offence, including whether committed alone or with associates, and whether these had been traced.
(f) *Judicial processes*: arrested or summonsed, police bail, details of all remands, reasons for remands, police objections to bail, bail amount/sureties, plea, offences taken into consideration, verdict and sentence.

The required information was collected from three main sources: (i) Police Charge Sheet, (ii) Court Papers, (iii) C. I. D. Crime Report File.

(i) The *Charge Sheet* provided relevant details of personal identification, date and time of arrest, full charge, police bail, remands and results of the case.

(ii) The *Court Papers* usually included the following: character and 'antecedents' of the defendant, prepared by the police; witnesses' statements; account by the arresting and/or investigating officer; defendant's statement; photographs of injuries etc. and a doctor's report on their extent. In the urban court, the first sheet of the Court Papers was invaluable, as it gave brief details of police reasons for remand requests, whether the remand was on bail or in custody, and (where applicable) police objections to bail. It was a great loss to the research that similar information was not available for the rural cases.

(iii) The C. I. D. *Crime Report File* included the main Crime Report form, giving full details of the offence, *modus operandi*, and what proceedings were taken by the police against whom; the initial Crime Complaint form; full details of all the property which was the subject of the charge or inquiry; forensic reports; official form of offences taken into consideration; miscellaneous correspondence; and the Supplementary Crime Report, by the C. I. D. officer in charge of the investigation, being a continuous report of the development of inquiries, and a valuable source of information about police reasons for remands, and manoeuvrings concerning bail.

The process of consulting these documentary sources of evidence was very much simpler and more convenient for the urban cases, where all the police files, charge sheets etc., were kept in the central police headquarters, than for the rural cases, where the files were scattered in several different places. All the documentary work on the urban cases was completed during the three-month period when observation was taking place in the magistrates' courts; the usual pattern of work was observation in the court during the morning and early afternoon, and work on documents during the remaining hours when the court was not sitting.

The same procedure for collecting information for the rural cases necessarily had to be spread over a much longer, twelve-month period; three separate court registers were consulted, and three separate police headquarters visited for the Charge Sheets and Files; in addition, many of the C.I.D. Crime Report Files had to be requested from the County Police Headquarters. It was not as possible to combine this documentary work with the court observation, and the average time for each case was very much longer than in the urban court. Unfortunately, also, the information in the files was neither as consistent nor as comprehensive as in the urban cases, and this vitiated many of the comparisons which it had been hoped to make between the two samples.

Court observation

The business of the urban court was distributed among several separate benches of magistrates in daily session. Indictable offences were normally heard in the two main courts, No. 1 Court and No. 2 Court; the distribution of cases between these two courts was determined by several factors of policy and administrative convenience, but, as a rule, all those persons who had been arrested, and were facing police charges, appeared in No. 1 Court. In fact, during the period of observation, 77 per cent of persons charged with indictable offences appeared in this court.

No. 1 Court sat on every day of the week, Monday to Saturday, but usually managed to dispose of its business without prolonging its sitting into the afternoon; as it was decided that all observation should take place in this main court, most afternoons were available for collecting material for the sample of documentary cases, which proved to be a most economical arrangement for the purposes of the research time-table.

The observation in No. 1 Court extended over a consecutive period of nine weeks, 30th June—28th August, 1965, during which the court was attended each day, for six days a week. During this period 128 remands before trial were observed, involving a total of 99 persons. No committal proceedings could be attended, as they were held in a different court.

The observation at the rural court extended over a longer period than at the urban court, in order to include an adequate number of remand decisions. Each court normally sat on only one day of the week; Courts (i) and (ii) on Wednesdays, and Court (iii) on Thursdays. Courts (i) and (iii) usually divided the magistrates into two separate benches in order to expedite business, especially when there were any committal proceedings. Court (ii) was unable to operate this arrangement, because of a shortage of clerical staff at that time. Because of the relative infrequency of indictable offences and of remands, it was possible to attend practically every remand decision (including committal proceedings) in these rural courts.

Periods of attendance were as follows:

Court (*i*): Wednesday, 20th April—Wednesday, 17th August, 1966; Fifteen sessions were attended, one session was missed. On two weeks there was no magistrates' court, as the Quarter Sessions and Assizes were sitting.

Court (*ii*): Wednesday, 14th September—Wednesday, 21st December, 1966; all thirteen sessions were attended. Quarter Sessions were sitting on two weeks.

Court (*iii*): Thursday, 21st April—Thursday, 22nd December, 1966; Thirty-two sessions were attended, including one 'occasional court'; five sessions were missed.

Combining the periods of observation at all three courts, a total of sixty court sessions were attended and forty-three remands before trial were witnessed, involving forty-one persons.

Although attendance at magistrates' courts is open to the general public, it was thought proper to contact the Clerk to the Justices and the Probation Department responsible to each court, before embarking upon these periods of extended observation. The fullest cooperation was obtained and facilities were provided for the author to sit in that part of the court which is reserved for members of the Probation Service; this was usually in the well of the court, and was therefore very convenient for observing the minutiae of court procedure.

A copy of the court agenda was usually provided shortly before the session, so that during the remand hearings attention could be paid to recording the details of procedure. Comprehensive notes were made on all cases involving remands, including a verbatim record of what was said by the various parties in the case. Pilot work had shown that it was quite possible to take comprehensive notes of this kind, especially as the majority of decisions were reached within a very few minutes. No standard format was used for the purposes of recording the information, because this might have resulted in certain important omissions; instead, a complete record was kept, and selection of the material was made at a later stage of the analysis.

REFERENCES

ARCHBOLD (1966). *Pleading, Evidence and Practice in Criminal Cases.* 36th ed. London.

ARES, C. E. AND STURZ, H. J. (1962). 'Bail and the Indigent Accused'. *Crime and Delinquency, 8,* 1.

ARES, C. E., RANKIN, A. AND STURZ, H. J. (1963). 'The Manhattan Bail Project: An Interim Report on the Use of Pre-trial Release.' 38 *N.Y.U.L. Rev.* 67.

BOTTOMLEY, A. K. (1968). 'The Granting of Bail: Principles and Practice.' 31 *Modern Law Review,* 40.

BOTTOMLEY, A. K. (1969). 'Custodial Remands: a Study of Policy and Practice in Magistrates' Courts.' Unpublished Ph.D. thesis, Cambridge University Library.

CHAPPELL, D. (1965). 'The Development and Administration of the English Law relating to Offences of Breaking and Entering.' Unpublished Ph.D. thesis, Cambridge University Library.

DAVIES, C. (1968). 'Imprisonment before Sentence.' Unpublished M.A. thesis, Liverpool University Library.

DEVLIN, P. (1960). *The Criminal Prosecution in England.* London.

DU CANE, E. (1885). *The Punishment and Prevention of Crime.* London.

FOOTE, C. (1958). 'Foreword: Comment on the New York Bail Study.' 106 *U.Pa.L.Rev.* 685.

FOOTE, C. (1965). 'The Coming Constitutional Crisis in Bail.' 113 *U.Pa.L.Rev.* 959, 1125.

FOOTE, C. (ed.) (1966). *Studies on Bail.* University of Pennsylvania.

FOOTE, C. et al. (1960). 'Conditional Release Pending Trial: A Symposium.' 108 *U.Pa.L.Rev.* 290.

FOOTE, C. MARKLE, J. P. AND WOLLEY, E. A. (1954). 'Compelling Appearance in Court: Administration of Bail in Philadelphia.' 102 *U.Pa.L.Rev.* 1031.

FREED, D. J. AND WALD, P. M. (1964) *Bail in the United States: 1964.* Washington, D.C.

FRIEDLAND, M. L. (1965). *Detention Before Trial.* University of Toronto.

Goldfarb, R. L. (1965). *Ransom: A Critique of the American Bail System*. New York.

Grünhut, M. (1956). *Juvenile Offenders before the Courts*. Oxford.

Hogarth, J. (1967a). 'Sentencing Research—Some Problems of Design.' *Brit. J. Crim. 7*, 1.

Hogarth, J. (1967b). 'Towards the Improvement of Sentencing in Canada.' *Can. Jo. Corr. 9*, 122.

Home Office (1960). *Prisons and Borstals*. London.

Home Office. *Judicial Statistics, England and Wales*, 1857–1893. London.

Home Office. *Criminal Statistics, England and Wales*. 1894–1968. London.

Home Office. *Reports of the Commissioners of Prisons*. 1878–1962. London.

Home Office. *Reports on the Work of the Prison Department*. 1963–69. London.

Home Office. *Reports on the Work of the Prison Department: Statistical Tables*. 1962–68. London.

Home Office Research Unit (1960). *Time Spent Awaiting Trial*. London.

Hood, R. G. (1962). *Sentencing in Magistrates' Courts*. London.

Hood, R. G. (1966). 'Research on the Sentencing of Motoring Offenders in Magistrates' Courts.' Unpublished paper, Second National Conference on Research and Teaching in Criminology, Cambridge, June 1966.

Howard, J. (1877). *The State of the Prisons*. London.

'Justice' (1966). *Interim Report of Joint Working Party on Bail and Remands in Custody*. London.

McClintock, F. H. assisted by Avison, N. H. (1963). *Crimes of Violence*. London.

Mannheim, H. and Wilkins, L. T. (1955). *Prediction Methods in Relation to Borstal Training*. London.

Mostyn, F. E. (1964). 'Bail and the Presumption of Innocence: England and America—a Comparison.' *Law Society's Gazette, 61*, 12, 799.

Napley, D. (1967). *A Guide to Law and Practice under the Criminal Justice Act, 1967*. London.

Patchett, K. W. and McClean, J. D. (1965). 'Decision-making in Juvenile Cases.' [1965] *Crim. L. R.* 699.

Pugh, R. B. (1968). *Imprisonment in Mediaeval England*. London

Rankin, A. (1964). 'The Effect of Pre-trial Detention.' 39 *N.Y.U.L.Rev.* 641.

Roberts, J. W. and Palermo, J. S. (1958). 'A Study of the Administration of Bail in New York.' 106 *U.Pa.L.Rev.* 685.

Sparks, R. F. (1965). 'Sentencing by Magistrates,' in Halmos, P. (Ed.) *Sociological Studies in the British Penal Services*. Keele.

Sturz, H. J. (1965). 'The Manhattan Bail Project and its Aftermath.' 27 *Am. Jo. Corr.* 6, 14.

Thomas, D. A. (1966). 'Police Powers II: Arrest—A General View.' [1966] *Crim. L.R.* 639.

U.S.A. (1965a). *Bail and Summons: 1965*. Washington, D.C.

U.S.A. (1965b). *National Conference on Bail and Criminal Justice: Proceedings of May 27–29, 1964, and Interim Report, May 1964—April, 1965.* Washington, D.C.

Wald, P. (1964). 'Pre-trial Detention and Ultimate Freedom: A Statistical Study.' 39 *N.Y.U.L. Rev.* 631.

Webb, S. and Webb, B. (1922). *English Prisons Under Local Government.* London.

Widgery Committee (1966). *Report of the Departmental Committee on Legal Aid in Criminal Proceedings.* Cmnd. 2934. London.

Wilkins, L. T. (1964). *Social Deviance.* London.

Zander, M. (1967). 'Bail: A Reappraisal.' [1967] *Crim. L.R.* 25, 100, 128.

C.